Cisco Networking Academy Program
IT Essentials I: PC Hardware and Software Supplement

Cisco Systems, Inc.

Cisco Networking Academy Program

Cisco Press

800 East 96th Street, 3rd Floor

Indianapolis, Indiana 46240 USA

www.ciscopress.com

Cisco Networking Academy Program
IT Essentials I: PC Hardware and Software Supplement

Cisco Systems, Inc.

Cisco Networking Academy Program

Course Sponsored by Hewlett-Packard Company

Copyright© 2004 Cisco Systems, Inc.

Published by:
Cisco Press
800 East 96th Street, 3rd Floor
Indianapolis, IN 46240 USA

ISBN: 1-58713-129-3

Printed in the United States of America 2 3 4 5 6 7 8 9 0

Second Printing   October 2003

Trademark Acknowledgments

All terms mentioned in this book that are known to be trademarks or service marks have been appropriately capitalized. Cisco Press or Cisco Systems, Inc. cannot attest to the accuracy of this information. Use of a term in this book should not be regarded as affecting the validity of any trademark or service mark.

Warning and Disclaimer

This book is designed to provide information about PC hardware and software. Every effort has been made to make this book as complete and as accurate as possible, but no warranty or fitness is implied.

The information is provided on an "as is" basis. The author, Cisco Press, and Cisco Systems, Inc., shall have neither liability nor responsibility to any person or entity with respect to any loss or damages arising from the information contained in this book or from the use of the discs or programs that may accompany it.

The opinions expressed in this book belong to the author and are not necessarily those of Cisco Systems, Inc.

This book is part of the Cisco Networking Academy® Program series from Cisco Press. The products in this series support and complement the Cisco Networking Academy Program curriculum. If you are using this book outside the Networking Academy program, then you are not preparing with a Cisco trained and authorized Networking Academy provider.

For information on the Cisco Networking Academy Program or to locate a Networking Academy, please visit www.cisco.com/edu.

Feedback Information

At Cisco Press, our goal is to create in-depth technical books of the highest quality and value. Each book is crafted with care and precision, undergoing rigorous development that involves the unique expertise of members from the professional technical community.

Readers' feedback is a natural continuation of this process. If you have any comments regarding how we could improve the quality of this book, or otherwise alter it to better suit your needs, you can contact us through e-mail at networkingacademy@ciscopress.com. Please make sure to include the book title and ISBN in your message.

We greatly appreciate your assistance.

Publisher	*John Wait*
Editor-in-Chief	*John Kane*
Cisco Representative	*Anthony Wolfenden*
Cisco Press Program Manager	*Sonia Torres Chavez*
Manager, Marketing Communications, Cisco Systems	*Scott Miller*
Cisco Marketing Program Manager	*Edie Quiroz*
Production Manager	*Patrick Kanouse*
Development Editor	*Sarah Kimberly*
Project Editor	*Sheri Cain*
Copy Editor	*Kris Simmons*
Technical Editors	*Frank Mann, David Planchard*
Designer	*Louisa Adair*
Composition	*Mark Shirar*
Indexer	*Tim Wright*

CISCO SYSTEMS

Corporate Headquarters
Cisco Systems, Inc.
170 West Tasman Drive
San Jose, CA 95134-1706
USA
www.cisco.com
Tel: 408 526-4000
800 553-NETS (6387)
Fax: 408 526-4100

European Headquarters
Cisco Systems International BV
Haarlerbergpark
Haarlerbergweg 13-19
1101 CH Amsterdam
The Netherlands
www-europe.cisco.com
Tel: 31 0 20 357 1000
Fax: 31 0 20 357 1100

Americas Headquarters
Cisco Systems, Inc.
170 West Tasman Drive
San Jose, CA 95134-1706
USA
www.cisco.com
Tel: 408 526-7660
Fax: 408 527-0883

Asia Pacific Headquarters
Cisco Systems, Inc.
Capital Tower
168 Robinson Road
#22-01 to #29-01
Singapore 068912
www.cisco.com
Tel: +65 6317 7777
Fax: +65 6317 7799

Cisco Systems has more than 200 offices in the following countries and regions. Addresses, phone numbers, and fax numbers are listed on the
Cisco.com Web site at www.cisco.com/go/offices.

Argentina • Australia • Austria • Belgium • Brazil • Bulgaria • Canada • Chile • China PRC • Colombia • Costa Rica • Croatia • Czech Republic Denmark • Dubai, UAE • Finland • France • Germany • Greece • Hong Kong SAR • Hungary • India • Indonesia • Ireland • Israel • Italy Japan • Korea • Luxembourg • Malaysia • Mexico • The Netherlands • New Zealand • Norway • Peru • Philippines • Poland • Portugal Puerto Rico • Romania • Russia • Saudi Arabia • Scotland • Singapore • Slovakia • Slovenia • South Africa • Spain • Sweden Switzerland • Taiwan • Thailand • Turkey • Ukraine • United Kingdom • United States • Venezuela • Vietnam • Zimbabwe

Overview

Table of Contents

Introduction

This supplement provides additional information on the Computer Technology Industry Association (CompTIA) A+ certification objectives and maintains compatibility with the latest revision of the IT Essential I: PC Hardware and Software course. It is to be used in conjunction with the existing *Cisco Networking Academy Program IT Essentials I: PC Hardware and Software Companion Guide* and online curriculum. This supplement covers additional and updated PC hardware and software concepts and technology and covers the additional key objectives of the CompTIA A+ exam, which is being updated with new testable objectives in the fall of 2003.

The majority of the existing *Cisco Networking Academy Program IT Essentials I: PC Hardware and Software Companion Guide* textbook content applies to the remaining and current CompTIA A+ certification objectives. However, this supplement adds specific A+ certification objectives to these chapters to enhance and broaden their scope. In addition, it provides some new information on some of the newest and latest PC hardware and software fundamentals, technologies, and subjects. It also includes new and updated labs that have been added to the curriculum. This supplement contains cross-references between its chapter information and the companion guide. This supplement is available to all the holders of the current *Cisco Networking Academy Program IT Essentials I: PC Hardware and Software Companion Guide.*

Guidelines for Use

Start by scanning the main headings in the supplemental chapters and note the cross-references to the chapters in the *Cisco Networking Academy Program IT Essentials I: PC Hardware and Software Companion Guide.* It is a good idea to make a note in the companion guide where you should insert the section of the supplement. When reading the companion guide, if you encounter a reference to the supplement, read the supplement section as well. Some chapters were left alone and none of the material was updated. However, some chapters included substantial enough changes that most or all of the chapter is included in its entirety. Therefore, read these chapters on their own as well as in the *Cisco Networking Academy Program IT Essentials I: PC Hardware and Software Companion Guide.* You can perform e-Labs using the online curriculum or the CD that comes with the companion guide. The course added new hands-on labs, and they appear in this exam supplement.

Description of Chapter Changes

The following is a brief description of changes made to each chapter in the IT Essentials I: PC Hardware and Software course. This section is a general overview of the changes.

Chapter 1: Information Technology Basics

The changes in this chapter were minor. Approximately 80 percent of this chapter is the same as in the companion guide. The supplement chapter includes many new figures that were updated to coincide with the updates required by A+ test objectives.

Chapter 2: How Computers Work

This chapter contains a number of changes to introduce new A+ test objectives. They include items such as portable and mobile technologies, the latest input devices, and cooling systems. This chapter also offers updates about some of the latest hardware standards, such as motherboards, CPUs, memory, and display devices.

Chapter 3: Assembling a Computer

This chapter has new figures to update and illustrate new topics in the latest A+ certification objectives, such as DVD-ROMs, towers, and computer cases. The new text is similar to the text in Chapter 3 of the companion guide with a few new paragraphs and sentences to reference the new material.

Chapter 6: Multimedia Capabilities

This chapter contains new graphics and text to include some of the latest multimedia technologies that are covered on the new A+ exam. They include some of the latest features of video cards, monitors, digital cameras and video recorders, and sound cards.

Chapter 10: Printers and Printing

This chapter includes additions to text and figures related to some of the printing objectives in the new A+ exam. It adds thermal and dye sublimation to the "Printing Overview" section. This chapter also includes a new section on the latest methods to upgrade printer components such as trays, feeders, and finishers. The chapter includes new material on upgrading or troubleshooting scanners, copiers, and fax machines.

Chapter 11: Preventive Maintenance

This chapter provides additional general information on preventative maintenance methods. Most importantly, it includes new material on firewalls and using firewalls to protect computer systems and networks.

Chapter 13: Troubleshooting Software

This chapter adds new figures and text about troubleshooting new operating systems such as Windows XP, which was added to the CompTIA A+ test objectives.

Windows XP Operating System Addendum

This chapter is included in its entirety because it does not appear in the current *IT Essentials I Companion Guide*. Many of the new A+ test objectives cover much Windows XP material. Most of this material is included in this new chapter.

Windows XP Operating System Labs

This chapter includes new hands-on labs that supplement the text and online curriculum.

Summary of Changes

Table I-1 highlights the key changes and updates that are covered in this supplement and how they map to the Cisco Networking Academy Program online curriculum.

Table I-1 IT Essentials I: PC Hardware and Software Companion Guide and Supplement Map

Companion Guide Chapters and Materials	Supplement Chapters and Materials	Corresponding Online Chapter and Materials
1, Information Technology Basics	1, Information Technology Basics No lab changes between companion guide and online curriculum.	1, Information Technology Basics
2, How Computers Work Worksheet 2.3.1: PC Power Supply Lab 2.3.2: Motherboard Identification Lab 2.3.4: Identify ROM and BIOS Chips Worksheet 2.3.4: BIOS/ROM Lab 2.3.6: Identifying Computer Expansion Slots Worksheet 2.3.5: Identifying Computer Expansion Slots Lab 2.3.7: Identifying RAM and RAM Sockets Worksheet 2.3.7: RAM and RAM Sockets Lab 2.3.9: Video Card Identification Worksheet 2.3.9: Video Cards Worksheet 2.3.13: Floppy Drive Worksheet 2.3.14: Hard Drive Identification Worksheet 2.3.15: CD-ROM Identification	2, How Computers Work	2, How Computers Work Worksheet 2.3.1: PC Power Supply Lab 2.3.6: Motherboard Identification Lab 2.3.8: Identify ROM and BIOS Chips Worksheet 2.3.8: BIOS/ROM Lab 2.3.9: Identifying Computer Expansion Slots Worksheet 2.3.9: Expansion Slots Lab 2.4.2: Identifying RAM and RAM Sockets Worksheet 2.4.2: RAM and RAM Sockets Lab 2.5.2: Video Card Identification Worksheet 2.5.2: Video Cards Worksheet 2.7.1: Floppy Drive Worksheet 2.7.2: Hard Drive Identification Worksheet 2.7.3: CD-ROM Identification

continues

Table I-1 IT Essentials I: PC Hardware and Software Companion Guide and Supplement Map (Continued)

Companion Guide Chapters and Materials	Supplement Chapters and Materials	Corresponding Online Chapter and Materials
3, Assembling a Computer	3, Assembling a Computer No lab changes between companion guide and online curriculum.	3, Assembling a Computer
4, Operating System Fundamentals	Chapter 4 is not needed in the supplement. No lab changes between companion guide and online curriculum.	4, Operating System Fundamentals
5, Windows 9x Operating Systems	Chapter 5 is not needed in the supplement. No lab changes between companion guide and online curriculum.	5, Windows 9x Operating Systems
6, Multimedia Capabilities Lab 6.2.3: Upgrading the Video Accelerator Lab 6.3.4: Sound Card Installation Worksheet 6.1.6: Multimedia Devices Worksheet 6.2.5: Video Accelerators Worksheet 6.3.3: Sound Cards Worksheet 6.4.7: CD and DVD Terminology	6, Multimedia Capabilities	Chapter 8: Windows NT/2000/XP Operating Systems Lab 8.2.3: Upgrading the Video Accelerator Lab 8.3.4: Sound Card Installation Worksheet 8.1.6: Multimedia Devices Worksheet 8.2.5: Video Accelerators Worksheet 8.3.3: Sound Cards Worksheet 8.4.7: CD and DVD Terminology
7, Windows NT/2000/XP Operating Systems Lab 7.1.2: Assigning Permissions in Windows 2000 Lab 7.2.1: Creating User Accounts in Windows 2000 Lab 7.2.4: Creating User Accounts in Windows 2000 Lab 7.3.1: Installation Demonstration of Windows 2000	Chapter 7 is not needed in the supplement.	6, Windows NT/2000/XP Operating Systems Lab 6.1.2: Assigning Permissions in Windows 2000 Lab 6.2.1: Creating User Accounts in Windows 2000 Lab 6.2.4: Creating User Accounts in Windows 2000 Lab 6.3.1: Installation Demonstration of Windows 2000
8, Advanced Hardware Fundamentals for Servers Lab 8.1.2: Basic Disk to Dynamic Disk Conversion Worksheet 8.1.3: RAID Worksheet 8.4.3: Adding Processors Worksheet 8.5.3: Adapters	Chapter 8 is not needed in the supplement.	9, Advanced Hardware Fundamentals for Servers Lab 9.1.2: Basic Disk to Dynamic Disk Conversion Worksheet 9.1.3: RAID Worksheet 9.4.4: Adding Processors Worksheet 9.5.3: Adapters

Table I-1 IT Essentials I: PC Hardware and Software Companion Guide and Supplement Map (Continued)

Companion Guide Chapters and Materials	Supplement Chapters and Materials	Corresponding Online Chapter and Materials
9, Networking Fundamentals Lab 9.3.1: NIC Installation Lab 9.3.3: Configuring the NIC to Work with the DHCP Server Lab 9.7.2: Troubleshooting the NIC Using the Ping Command Worksheet 9.2.5: Types of Networks Worksheet 9.4.2: Network Topology Worksheet 9.6.5: OSI Model, TCP/IP, Protocols Worksheet 9.8.7: Connecting to the Internet	Chapter 9 is not needed in the supplement.	10, Networking Fundamentals Lab 10.3.1: NIC Installation Lab 10.3.3: Configuring the NIC to Work with the DHCP Server Lab 10.7.2: Troubleshooting the NIC Using the Ping Command Worksheet 10.2.5: Types of Networks Worksheet 10.4.2: Network Topology Worksheet 10.6.5: OSI Model, TCP/IP, Protocols Worksheet 10.8.7: Connecting to the Internet
10, Printers and Printing Lab 10.3.8: Adding an Ink Jet Printer to Your Computer Lab 10.4.4: Setting Up Print Sharing Capabilities Lab 10.5.4: Managing Files in a Printer Queue Lab 10.6.1: Paper Jams	10, Printers and Printing	11, Printers and Printing Lab 11.3.7: Adding an Ink Jet Printer to Your Computer Lab 11.4.4: Setting Up Print Sharing Capabilities Lab 11.5.4: Managing Files in a Printer Queue Lab 11.6.1: Paper Jams
11, Preventive Maintenance Lab 11.1.2: Using a Digital Multimeter Lab 11.3.5: Cleaning Computer Components Lab 11.4.1: Using the Scandisk and Defrag Utilities Worksheet 11.1.3: Environmental Considerations Worksheet 11.2.1: Electrostatic Discharge Worksheet 11.3.5: Preventative Maintenance for Components	11, Preventive Maintenance	12, Preventive Maintenance and Upgrading Lab 12.1.2: Using a Digital Multimeter Lab 12.3.5: Cleaning Computer Components Lab 12.4.1: Using the Scandisk and Defrag Utilities Worksheet 12.1.4: Environmental Considerations Worksheet 12.2.1: Electrostatic Discharge Worksheet 12.3.5: Preventative Maintenance for Components

continues

Table I-1 IT Essentials I: PC Hardware and Software Companion Guide and Supplement Map (Continued)

Companion Guide Chapters and Materials	Supplement Chapters and Materials	Corresponding Online Chapter and Materials
12, Troubleshooting PC Hardware Lab 12.1.7: The Steps of the Troubleshooting Cycle Lab 12.2.3: Identifying POST Errors Worksheet 12.1.2: Troubleshooting Basics Worksheet 12.3.2: Troubleshooting Printers Worksheet 12.3.4: Troubleshooting Hardware	Chapter 9 is not needed in the supplement.	13, Troubleshooting PC Hardware Lab 13.1.7: The Steps of the Troubleshooting Cycle Lab 13.2.2: Identifying POST Errors Worksheet 13.1.2: Troubleshooting Basics Worksheet 13.3.2: Troubleshooting Printers Worksheet 13.3.4: Troubleshooting Hardware
13, Troubleshooting Software Lab 13.7.4: Booting into Safe Mode Lab 13.7.5: Using the Windows 2000 Recovery Console Lab 13.9.3: Windows Registry Backup and Recovery Worksheet 13.4.5: Troubleshooting Software	13, Troubleshooting Software	14, Troubleshooting Software Lab 14.7.4: Booting into Safe Mode Lab 14.7.5: Using the Windows 2000 Recovery Console Lab 14.10.3: Windows Registry Backup and Recovery Worksheet 14.4.5: Troubleshooting Software
	Windows XP Operating System Addendum Lab 7.3.2: Installation Demonstration of Windows XP Lab 7.5.2: Using Simple File Sharing to Share Files Lab 7.5.3a: Remote Desktop Connection Lab 7.5.3b: Internet Connection Firewall Lab 7.5.5: Using Windows XP Start Menu and Windows Explorer	7, Windows XP Operating System Lab 7.3.2: Installation Demonstration of Windows XP Lab 7.5.2: Using Simple File Sharing to Share Files Lab 7.5.3a: Remote Desktop Connection Lab 7.5.3b: Internet Connection Firewall Lab 7.5.5: Using Windows XP Start Menu and Windows Explorer

Chapter 1

Information Technology Basics

This chapter discusses the basics of information technology (IT) as they relate to the computer technician. It covers different computer types and software applications. It also includes a brief overview of the Internet. You will identify the basic features of the Windows operating system and the elements of the Windows desktop.

Additionally, you will learn several vocabulary words that are important to the technician. You will also examine the methods used in number conversions, including binary to decimal and decimal to binary. This chapter also includes an explanation of analog and digital as well as an introduction to algorithms.

The first priority in working with computers is safety. This chapter details safety procedures that pertain to the labs used throughout this course and in the workplace.

Computer Systems and Programs

A computer system, as shown in Figure 1-1, consists of hardware and software components. *Hardware* is the physical equipment, such as the case, floppy disk drives, keyboards, monitors, cables, speakers, and printers. The term *software* describes the programs that you use to operate the computer system. Computer software, also called *programs*, instructs the computer on how to operate. These operations can include identifying, accessing, and processing information. Essentially, a program is a sequence of instructions that describe how data is to be processed. Programs vary widely, depending on the type of information that is to be accessed or generated. For example, the instructions involved in balancing a checkbook are very different from those required to simulate a virtual-reality world on the Internet.

Figure 1-1 Computer System

The two types of software are operating systems and applications.

Application software accepts input from the user and then manipulates it to achieve a result, known as the *output*. Applications are programs designed to perform a specific function directly for the user or for another application program. Examples of applications include word processors, database programs, spreadsheets, web browsers, web development tools, and graphic design tools. Computer applications are detailed later in this chapter. See Figures 1-2, 1-3, and 1-4 for examples of common application software.

Figure 1-2 Microsoft Word Application

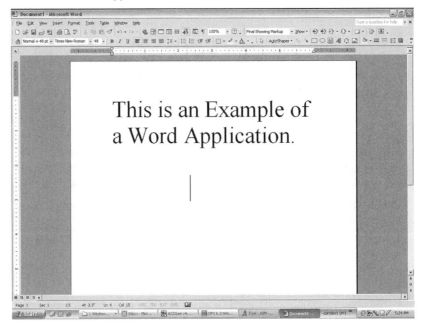

Figure 1-3 Microsoft Excel Application

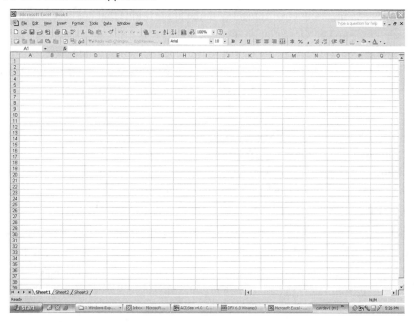

Figure 1-4 Microsoft PowerPoint Application

An operating system (OS) is a program that manages all the other programs in a computer. It also provides the operating environment with the applications that are used to access resources on the computer. Operating systems perform basic tasks such as recognizing input from the keyboard or mouse, sending output to the video screen or printer, keeping track of files on the drives, and controlling peripherals such as printers and modems. The Disk Operating System (DOS), Windows 98, Windows 2000, Windows NT, Linux, Mac OS X, DEC VMS, and IBM OS/400 are all examples of operating systems.

Operating systems are platform-specific, meaning they are designed for uses with different types of computers. For example, the Windows operating system (3.1, 95, 98, 2000, XP, or NT) is designed for use with an IBM-compatible personal computer, often referred to as a PC. The Mac OS, on the other hand, will only work with Macintosh computers. PC and Macintosh are called platforms. A platform is the computer system on which programs can run.

Firmware is basically a program that is embedded in a silicon chip rather than stored on a floppy disk. Any change to either the hardware or software can cause firmware to become outdated, leading to device or system failure or even data loss. When this happens to older firmware, the only solution is to replace it. Current firmware is flashable, meaning that the contents can be upgraded or flashed. This subject is covered in more depth in a later chapter.

Computer Types

This section details two types of computers. The first is the *mainframe*, which has provided computing power for major corporations for more than 40 years. The second is the *personal computer*, which has had more impact on people and business than any other device in history.

Mainframes

Mainframes are powerful machines that allow companies to automate manual tasks, shorten marketing time for new products, use financial models that enhance profitability, and so on. The mainframe model consists of centralized computers that are usually housed in secure, climate-controlled computer rooms. End users interface with the computers through dumb terminals. These terminals are low-cost devices that usually consist of a monitor, keyboard, and a communication port to communicate with the mainframe. Initially, terminals were hard-wired directly to communication ports on the mainframe and the communications were asynchronous. Figure 1-5 is an illustration of a mainframe computer.

Figure 1-5 A Mainframe Computer

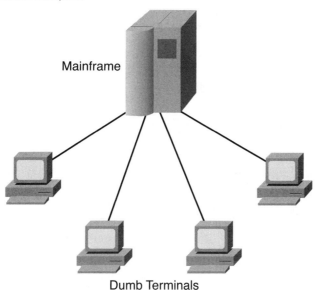

Mainframe

Dumb Terminals

NOTE

Asynchronous means without respect to time. In terms of data transmission, asynchronous means that no clock or timing source is needed to keep both the sender and the receiver synchronized. Without the use of a clock, the sender must signal the start and stop of each character so the receiver will know when to expect data.

A mainframe environment consists of a single computer or group of computers that can be centrally managed and maintained. This configuration has the additional advantage of being more secure for two reasons. First, the computer is stored in a secure room. Second, the end user's ability to introduce viruses into the system is decreased. Virus protection and eradication costs companies hundreds of millions of U.S. dollars annually.

At its peak in the late 1970s and early 1980s, the mainframe and minicomputer market was dominated by IBM and Digital Equipment Corporation. The minicomputer was a smaller and less expensive line of mainframes. However, these high-powered machines came with high price tags. The cost of entry into the mainframe market was typically several hundred thousand to several million U.S. dollars. The minicomputer began to bring similar capabilities at a lower price, but the minicomputer configurations often cost more than 10,000 U.S. dollars.

Mainframes continue to be prominent in corporate computing. It is estimated that 24 million dumb terminals are currently in use worldwide. In addition, 15 million PCs are currently deployed to function primarily as mainframe terminal emulators. These dumb terminals are American Standard Code for Information Interchange (ASCII) character-based devices. They are often referred to as green screens because many display green characters.

The term mainframe used to refer to the cabinet that housed the CPU. Today, it refers to a large computer system.

There are several advantages to mainframes:

- Scalability (the ability to add more users as the need arises)
- Centralized management
- Centralized backup
- Low-cost desktop devices (dumb terminals)
- High level of security

There are several disadvantages to mainframes:

- Character-based applications
- Lack of vendor operating-system standards and interoperability in multivendor environments
- Expensive maintenance, initial equipment, and setup
- Potential for a single point of failure in non fault-tolerant configurations
- Potential for a bottleneck in timesharing systems

PCs

A personal computer (PC) is a standalone device. This means that it is independent of all other computers, as shown in Figure 1-6. With the advent of the PC, the graphical user interface (GUI) gained wide introduction to users.

Figure 1-6 Personal Computer

A GUI, pronounced goo-ee, employs a graphics display to represent procedures and programs that can be executed by the computer. An example is the Windows desktop, as shown in Figure 1-7. These programs routinely use small pictures, called *icons*, to represent different programs. The advantage of using a GUI is that the user does not have to remember complicated commands to execute a program. The GUIs first appeared in Xerox and Apple computers. Along with GUI, thousands of Windows-based applications were also introduced.

Figure 1-7 Windows GUI Example

As PC technology has improved, the power of the PC has risen to the point that it can perform enterprise-level functions.

There are several advantages to PC computing:

- Standardized hardware
- Standardized, highly interoperable operating systems
- GUI interface
- Low-cost devices and low cost of entry, when compared to mainframes
- Distributed computing
- User flexibility
- High-productivity applications

There are several disadvantages to PC computing:

- High cost for a desktop computer, which averages five times the cost of a dumb terminal, according to some industry estimates
- No centralized backup
- No centralized management
- Physical, data access, and virus security risks can be greater
- High management and maintenance costs, which are generally cheaper than for mainframes

The Cost of Technology: More and More for Less and Less

As computer and networking technology has advanced over the past few decades, the cost of the increasingly sophisticated technology has fallen dramatically. Those falling prices are partially responsible for the rising prominence of connectivity solutions in the business world and in personal lives.

In the 1970s and 1980s, the PC shown in Figure 1-8 was considered the best available at the time, and it cost several thousand U.S. dollars. Online services existed. However, only big businesses and the wealthy could afford them at the cost of 25 U.S. dollars or more per hour of access. PC veterans can still remember the announcement of the Prodigy bargain rates of only 9.95 U.S. dollars an hour for online access. The available speeds were 1200 or 2400 baud, which would be considered unusable by the current user.

Figure 1-8 A Legacy PC

For example, a user can buy a computer system in the United States for under 1000 U.S. dollars that is capable of doing much more. Such a machine could also operate better and faster than the mainframe version of 20 years ago, which cost 500,000 U.S. dollars. Figure 1-9 shows an example of a modern PC. Internet access at speeds equivalent to T1 is available through digital subscriber line (DSL) or cable modem service for 30 to 40 U.S. dollars per month, and prices are continually decreasing. You can obtain basic Internet access at 56 kbps for much less, even free, if you can tolerate additional advertising on the screen.

Figure 1-9 A Modern PC

Chapter 2

How Computers Work

Input, Process, Output, and Storage

As mentioned in the previous chapter, the operating system (OS) is the software that controls functionality and provides lower-level routines for application programs. Most operating systems provide functions to read and write data to files. An OS translates requests for operations on files into operations that the disk controller can carry out. The OS helps the computer perform the following four basic operations, as shown in Figure 2-1.

Figure 2-1 An Input Device

- The input operation recognizes input from the keyboard or mouse.
- The processing operation manipulates data according to the user's instructions.
- The output operation sends output to the video screen or printer.
- The storage operation keeps track of files for use later. Examples of storage devices include floppy disks and hard drives.

The most common way to input data into a computer is with a keyboard and mouse, as shown in Figure 2-2. Another way to input data is with a touch screen. Touch screens (as shown in Figure 2-3) on full-size computers have on-screen buttons that you can access with a finger or a stylus. These applications are custom-designed and typically very simple so anyone can use them. Personal digital assistants (PDAs) and tablet computers also use touch screens where a stylus is required for precise interaction with screen objects. Input devices allow you to navigate the computer to open a web page, send an e-mail file, or access a file from a network server. After the data is input, the computer can process or crunch the data. While a file is open and the text is being reformatted, the computer is processing data.

Figure 2-2 Keyboard and Mouse

Figure 2-3 Touch Screen

Processing data usually results in some kind of output, such as a word-processor file or a spreadsheet. The most common way to output data is to send it to the computer monitor, as shown in Figure 2-4, or to a printer. Today, most computers have a connection to the Internet, making it common to output the data to the Internet via e-mail or as a web page.

Figure 2-4 Computer Monitor

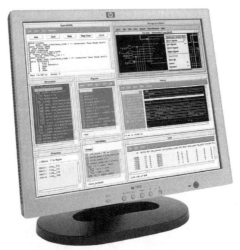

Data storage is probably the most important of the four basic computer functions. The most common way to store a file is to save it to a hard drive. You can think of hard drives as very large file cabinets. An operating system finds a place on the hard drive, saves the file, and remembers its location.

Computer Cases and Power Supplies

The computer case and the power supply are two important parts that help determine the performance of the system. The type of motherboard is usually determined by the type of case and power supply. (The power supply is usually included in the computer case.) This section details computer cases and power supplies.

Computer Cases

The type of case is the first decision when building a computer.   The case consists of the metal chassis (or frame) and a cover, usually constructed of metal or hard plastic. The case is the housing unit for the internal components and protects against dust and damage. The case usually comes with the power supply needed to power the computer and the installed components. Computer cases are either desktop or tower models, as shown in Figure 2-5 and Figure 2-6.

Figure 2-5 Desktop Computer Model

Figure 2-6 Tower Computer Model

The desktop model sits on a desk horizontally. The monitor can sit on top. This choice can be a space-saver. The tower model stands upright in a vertical position that allows easy placement on the floor. Mini-tower, mid-tower, and full-tower cases are available.

The choice of a desktop case or tower is a matter of personal preference. However, it is important to consider the workspace before choosing a case.

Hardware components are installed in the bays of the case. The bays are placeholders for the drives so they are neatly organized. You can easily interchange devices from bay to bay if necessary. Drive bays are 5.25 inches or 3.5 inches wide, and a new computer usually leaves some unfilled. The empty slots let you upgrade the machine with a Zip drive, tape back-up, or CD-ROM burner.

Tables 2-1 and 2-2 summarize information about the different parts of a typical computer case and indicate the factors to consider when selecting a case.

Table 2-1 Typical Parts of a Computer Case

Part	Purpose
Frame	The main board and all the objects inside and outside are attached to the frame. The frame is what defines the computer's size and shape.
Cover panels	These panels attach to the frame to enclose all the parts of the PC. It is not advisable to operate the computer without the cover panels in place because they are instrumental in protecting the parts, directing airflow to cool the circuits, and containing the radio frequency interference (RFI) and EMI emissions of the power-supply unit.

Table 2-1 Typical Parts of a Computer Case (Continued)

Part	Purpose
LED and button connectors	These connect the buttons and LEDs on the front of the case to the motherboard.
Speaker and connector	The speaker connects to the motherboard and provides a very basic way to diagnose startup problems.
I/O template	This metal template on the back of the case provides access holes to the motherboard's peripheral connectors. On some cases, you can replace the template to provide the correct access holes depending on the main board's connector locations and spacing.
Expansion slots	You open these slots when you install an expansion card on the motherboard to provide access to the card's ports or connectors.
Case fan and connector	Most modern cases provide a secondary fan at the front of the unit to draw air in to circulate over the circuits and devices in the system. The fan connects to the main board to receive power.
5.25" drive bays	These are the large bays where you can install a 5.25" wide device, such as a CD-ROM drive. Usually, there is a plate or slot cover over the bay in the front that you must remove before the installation.
3.5" drive bays	These are the smaller bays where you can mount 3.5" devices, such as a floppy-disk or hard-disk drive. If you install a hard disk, you do not need to remove the slot cover because the disk is not removable.
Slot covers	You remove these covers when installing drive bays. Use the slot cover to protect the computer when the drive bay is not in use.
Vent holes	The design of the case dictates where the appropriate venting holes are placed. The manufacturer places these holes in the best possible place to ensure the correct airflow within the case.
Power supply mounting area	This area is for mounting the power supply unit if the case does not have one. Some cases come with a power supply already installed.
Front cover plate	This plate fits on the front of the case, providing a place for the LEDs and buttons, air intake control, and an aesthetically pleasing look.
Feet	The feet on the bottom of the case provide stability on uneven or slick surfaces. Some cases draw air from the very bottom of the case and the feet elevate the case to ensure proper airflow.

Table 2-2 Factors to Consider in Choosing a Computer Case

Factor	Rationale
Model type	There are four main case models. One type is for desktop PCs, and three types are for tower computers. The type of motherboard the user chooses determines the type of case. The size and shape must match exactly.
Size	The case should have enough space for the installed components. Additionally, there should be enough space to get to the components for service and for air to move across the components to dissipate the heat.
Available space	Desktop cases allow space conservation in tight areas because you can place the monitor on top of the unit. You can locate tower cases on or under the desk.
Number of devices	The more devices needing power in the system, the larger the power supply must be. This issue relates to the mounting area of the power supply in the case.
Power supply	Depending on the type of motherboard the user chose, the user must match the power rating and connection type to the power supply.
Environmental conditions	If the system will be in an area that is very dusty, it is a good idea to purchase a case designed to help reduce the amount of dust entering the system. Some cases offer easily replaceable filters for the case fan to trap dust.
Aesthetics	For some people, how the case looks doesn't matter at all. For others, it is critical. In case it is necessary to have a case that is attractive and aesthetically pleasing, a number of manufacturers consider this issue when designing a case.
Status display	What is going on inside the case can be very important. LED indicators that are mounted on the front of the case can tell the user whether the system is receiving power, when the hard drive is being used, and when the computer is on standby or sleeping.
Vents	All cases have a vent on the power supply, and some have another vent on the back to help draw air into or out of the system. Some cases are designed with more vents in case the system needs a way to dissipate an unusual amount of heat. This situation might occur when many devices are installed close together in the case.
Rigidity	When choosing a case, remember that the components inside are not designed to bend. The case should be sturdy enough to keep all the components inside from flexing.

Power Supplies

As shown in Figure 2-7, a power supply provides the voltage to power the various electronic circuits that make up the PC. It receives the external AC power.

Figure 2-7 External View of a Typical Power Supply

TIP

Alternating current (AC) flows in one direction and then reverses its direction and repeats the process. It is the most common form of electricity generated from a power plant. The power supply converts AC to direct current (DC) or other levels required for the system. DC is electrical current that travels in only one direction.

The power supply is contained in a metal box. Within this box, a transformer converts the voltage that is supplied from standard outlets into voltages that the computer parts need to operate.

A fan installed in the power supply prevents the computer and its components from overheating by maintaining an air flow. It is critical that these components be kept at a consistent operating temperature to ensure their best performance. The fan is built into the power supply with openings on the back side of the case. Never block or cover the fan inlet port.

There are several different types of power supplies, varying in size and design. The more common types are known as the AT and ATX power supply form factors. AT type supplies, which new systems no longer use, generally appear on computers built prior to the mid-1990s. ATX is the more common power supply. Probably the easiest way to distinguish the AT and ATX is by the nature of their connectors. Common PC power supplies are switched power supplies as opposed to linear power supplies.

The devices that attach to the power supply use +5v, +12v, and +3.3v DC power. Older devices (PC/XT and early AT) also use –5v and –12v DC power. The power supply must support the processor. Each power supply comes with all these specifications. Tables 2-3 and 2-4 describe the components of a typical ATX power supply and the factors you consider when selecting a power supply.

TIP

Power supplies are rated in watts. A typical computer has a 250–300 watt power supply.

Table 2-3 Components of a Power Supply

Part	Description
Case and cover	Isolate the power supply from the rest of the PC and keep electromagnetic emissions inside the unit.
Power cord	Connects the unit to a receptacle to supply AC power.

continues

Table 2-3 Components of a Power Supply (Continued)

Part	Description
Voltage selector switch	Allows the power supply to accept 110/120 volt, 60 Hz (North America) or 220/240 volt, 50 Hz AC power (outside North America). You can find more information at http://kropla.com/electric.htm.
Power switch	Before the ATX form factor, the power switch on the front of the system connected directly to the power supply in the case to switch power on and off.
Power converter	Converts AC to DC power for use within the PC.
Motherboard power connector	Supplies the necessary power to the motherboard.
Disk drive power connectors	Supplies the necessary power to the drives, auxiliary fans, and other devices inside the case.
Fan cooling system	Circulates air inside the case to keep the electronics and devices cool.
Fuse	Protects the power supply from damage if there is a power surge. The fuse will blow if it is subjected to too much current.

Table 2-4 Factors to Consider When Selecting a Power Supply

Factor	Rationale
Wattage	If you want to upgrade the PC with more equipment or faster processors, the power supply must provide enough power to the equipment without becoming overloaded.
Form factor	Depending on the type of case and motherboard, the power supply must adhere to the same form factor requirements to fit inside the case and correctly power the motherboard and other devices.
CPU type	Different CPUs require different voltages. For example, some AMD chips and motherboards might require more power than some Pentiums and vice versa.
Expandability	If the power supply only has enough power to supply the current CPU, motherboard, and devices, there might not be enough power to supply any upgrade to the system.

Table 2-4 Factors to Consider When Selecting a Power Supply (Continued)

Factor	Rationale
Energy efficiency	Each power supply has an efficiency rating. The higher this rating is, the less heat that is generated by the power supply when converting voltage.
Fan type and direction	It is important that the power supply have a high-quality fan. It is the primary source of airflow inside the case. Some fans can change direction to allow air to be blown directly on the CPU and to regulate the quality of the air entering the case.
Signals	The motherboard can regulate modern power supplies. The main board can regulate the speed of the fan, depending on the temperature inside the case. It can also turn off the fan to save power, and some "smart" power supplies can turn off the computer in the event of a fan failure before the components overheat.
Fault tolerance	If the user has a PC that needs to be on at all times, consider a dual power supply. If one of the units fails, the other one takes over right away. Some designs let you replace a power supply while the computer is still powered.
Line conditioning	One way to ensure that the DC voltages supplied to the PC are kept at normal levels when there are spikes or brownouts is to install a power supply that has built-in conditioning. These units ensure that the DC voltages supplied to the system remain stable even when the AC current coming in is not.

TIP

Electrical current, or current, is the flow of charges that is created when electrons move. In electrical circuits, current is caused by a flow of free electrons. When voltage (electrical pressure) is applied, and there is a path for the current, electrons move from the negative terminal (which repels them) along the path to the positive terminal (which attracts them).

Cooling Systems

As mentioned previously, the power supply fan helps prevent the computer components from overheating by maintaining an airflow in the case. Older computer cases could accommodate an additional fan (as shown in Figure 2-8), but now cases are designed to accommodate three, four, five, and even six additional fans.

Figure 2-8 Computer Case Fan

Overheating is a critical problem that can cause a computer system to malfunction or fail. A *heat sink* consists of a material that absorbs the heat generated and then disperses it away from the CPU. Chapter 3, "Assembling a Computer," covers installing a heat sink.

Other cooling methods are becoming more widely available. Although they are more expensive, computer cases made of aluminum create a much cooler environment for the installed components. Liquid cooled cases introduce water as a cooling agent. Liquid cooling units fit most cases that have a place to mount a back exhaust fan and include a pump, reservoir, the fan and radiator, and the CPU block. You can install and use the system to keep the components on an average of 8–10 degrees cooler.

The CPU or Processor

The CPU is one of the most important elements of the personal computer. On the motherboard, the CPU is contained on a single integrated circuit called the *microprocessor*. The computer will not run without a CPU. Often referred to as the brains of a computer, the CPU contains two basic components:

- A control unit instructs the rest of the computer system on how to follow a program instructions. It directs the movement of data to and from processor memory. The control unit temporarily holds data, instructions, and processed information in its arithmetic/logic unit (ALU). In addition, it directs control signals between the CPU and external devices such as hard disks, main memory, I/O ports, and so on.

- The ALU performs both arithmetic and logical operations. Arithmetic operations are fundamental math operations such as addition, subtraction, multiplication, and division. Logical operations such as AND, OR, and XOR make comparisons and decisions, which determine how a program is executed.

The processor handles most of the operations that are required of the computer by processing instructions and sending signals out, checking for connectivity, and ensuring that operations and hardware are functioning properly. It acts as a messenger to major components such as RAM, the monitor, and disk drives. The microprocessor is connected to the rest of the computer system through three buses, including the data bus, address bus, and control bus. (The bus types are discussed in detail later in this chapter.) Many different companies produce CPUs, including Intel, Advanced Micro Devices (AMD), and Cyrix. Intel is credited with making the first modern, silicon-based CPU chip in 1971.

Processor Socket Types

In dealing with microprocessors, you will encounter such terminology as Socket 7, Socket 370, Socket 423, or Slot1. Socket *x* (*x* being any number) is a descriptive term for the way certain processors plug into a computer motherboard so that they make contact with the built-in circuitry or data bus of the motherboard. Manufacturers can have different socket types for their processors. Socket 7, mostly outdated, is the best known of the major connection variations. It is used by some generation of each of the three major processor types: AMD, Intel, and Cyrix. Socket types with a larger number in the name are more current. For example, Socket 370 and higher are more current than anything lower. The progression from Socket 1 (Intel 486 processors) through Socket 423 (Intel Pentium 4 processors) has includes improved processor technology and speed. Table 2-5 summarizes the socket types and the different processor types that use them. You can find more information at http://www.firmware.com/support/bios/pentium.htm.

Table 2-5 CPU Socket Types

Socket Type	AMD	Intel
Socket 1	AM486DX-4, Am5x86	486SX/SX2, DX, DX2, DX4, Overdrive Processor
Socket 2	AM486DX-4, Am5x86	486SX/SX2, DX, DX2, DX4, Pentium Overdrive Processor
Socket 3	AM486DX-4, Am5x86	486SX/SX2, DX, DX2, DX4, Pentium Overdrive Processor
Socket 4		Pentium 60 MHz, Pentium 66 MHz, Pentium Overdrive 120–133 MHz
Socket 5	K5	Pentium 75–133 MHz, Pentium Overdrive 125–166, Pentium Overdrive MMX 125–180 MHz, Pentium MMX 166–200 MHz
Socket 6		The last 486 class socket standard created by Intel. modern motherboards do not use it.
Socket 7	K5, K6 166–300 MHz, K6-2 266–550 MHz, K6-3 400–450 MHz	Pentium 75–200 MHz, Pentium Overdrive 125–166 MHz, Pentium Overdrive MMX 125–200 MHz, Pentium MMX 166–233 MHz
Socket 8		Pentium Pro 150–200 MHz, Pentium II Overdrive 300–333 MHz
Slot 1		Celeron, Pentium II 233–450 MHz, Pentium III 450 MHz (and up).
Slot 2		Pentium II Xeon 400–450 MHz Pentium III Xeon 500 MHz – 1 GHz

continues

Table 2-5 CPU Socket Types (Continued)

Socket Type	AMD	Intel
Slot A	Athlon 500 MHz – 1 GHz	
Socket 370		Celeron, Pentium II 233–450 MHz, Pentium III 450 MHz – 1.13 GHz
Socket A	Duron 600 MHz +, Athlon 750 MHz +	
Socket 423		Pentium 4 1.3 GHz +
Socket 478		Pentium 4 1 GHz – 2.3 GHz +
Socket 603		Xeon 1 GHz – 1.4 GHz +

Socket 7 and other socket-type processors use the Zero Insertion Force (ZIF) socket. A ZIF socket is designed to allow the easy insertion of the microprocessor. A typical ZIF socket contains a lever that opens and closes, securing the microprocessor in place. Additionally, the various sockets have differing numbers of pins and pin-layout arrangements. Socket 7, for example, has 321 pins. The number of pins generally increases with the socket numbering.

Processor Slots

Slot-type processors had a brief lifespan (just about a year in the market). Intel, for its Pentium II processor, moved from the socket configuration to a processor packaged in a cartridge that fits into a slot in the motherboard. Similarly, AMD has progressed to Slot A (similar to Slot 1) and then to Socket A for its high-end AMD Athlon and Duron processors.

Pentium Processors

The current family of the Intel Pentium microprocessors includes the Pentium II, III, IV, and Xeon. The Pentium class is the current standard for processor chips. These processors represent the Intel processor second and third generations. By combining memory cache with microprocessor circuitry, the Pentium supports processor speeds of 1000 MHz and more. The combined chips cover less than 2 square inches (6 sq cm) and comprise over a million transistors.

The Pentium processors have made several improvements over their predecessor, which evolved from the Intel 80486. For instance, the Pentium data bus is 64 bits wide and can take in data 64 bits at a time, compared to 32 bits with the Intel 486. The Pentium has multiple caches of storage totaling as much as 2 MB compared to the 8 KB of the Intel 486.

Improvements in processor speeds allow the components to get data in and out of the chip more quickly. The processor does not become idle waiting for data or instructions, which enables the software to run faster. These components need to handle the flow of information through the processor, interpret instructions so the processor can execute them, and send the results back to the PC's memory. The manufacturer's website, http://www.intel.com, provides more information about the Pentium family of processors (P1, PII, PIII, PIV, and Xeon).

AMD Processors

The best performing AMD processors are the Athlon, Athlon XP, Thunderbird, and Duron series. They are currently the most used microprocessors, along with Intel Pentium IIIs, in high-end desktop systems, workstations, and servers. The AMD Athlon processor system bus is designed for scalable multiprocessing, with the number of AMD Athlon processors in a multiprocessor system determined by chipset implementation. The manufacturer's website, http://www.amd.com, provides more about the AMD family of processors (Athlons, Athlon XP, Thunderbird, and Durons).

Processor Speed Rating

CPU descriptions such as Pentium 133, Pentium 166, or Pentium 200 are well known. These numbers are specifications that indicate the maximum (reliable) operating speed at which the CPU can execute instructions. The CPU speed is not controlled by the microprocessor itself but by an external clock on the motherboard. The speed of the processor is determined by the frequency of the clock signal. It is typically expressed in megahertz (MHz), and the higher the number, the faster the processor. Processor speeds are getting faster all the time. Processor speeds of 3.0 GHz (3,000 MHz) are currently available.

The CPU speed and the frequency of the clock signal are not always at a one-to-one ratio. The CPU can run at a much higher MHz than the other chips on the motherboard. A variable-frequency synthesizer circuit built into the motherboard circuit multiplies the clock signal so that the motherboard can support several speeds of CPUs. Generally, three factors determine how much information can be processed at any given time:

- The size of the internal bus
- The size of the address bus
- The processor's speed ratings

Expansion Slots

Expansion slots, also known as *sockets*, are receptacles on the computer motherboard that accept printed circuit boards. All computers have expansion slots that let you add devices. Video cards, I/O cards, and sound cards are examples of components in expansion slots.

There are several types of expansion slots on a motherboard. The number and type of expansion slots in the computer determine future expansion possibilities. Figure 2-9 shows the different slot types, and Table 2-6 summarizes some useful information on the more common slot types and others that have never gained widespread use in the industry.

Figure 2-9 Expansion Slot Types

Table 2-6 Expansion Slots

Slot Type	Speed (MHz)	Data Bits	Use
Industry Standard Architecture (ISA)	4.77, 8	8, 16	Modems, 8-bit expansion cards.
MCA	10	32	This bus is obsolete.
Extended ISA (EISA)	8	8, 16, 32	Specialty roles, mostly obsolete and being replaced by PCI in new systems.
VESA Local	33	32, 64	Once used for faster video performance than the ISA bus. This bus has since become obsolete.
Peripheral Component Interconnect (PCI)	33	32, 64	Audio and video cards, networking cards, modems, SCSI adapters, and more. Not for use with serial or parallel ports.
Accelerated Graphics Port (AGP)	66	32	Video adapter only.

Common expansion slots include the following:

- The ISA is a 16-bit expansion slot developed by IBM. It transfers data with the motherboard at 8 MHz. ISA slots are becoming obsolete and are being replaced by PCI slots in new systems. However, many motherboard manufacturers might still include one or two for backward compatibility with older expansion cards. In 1987, IBM introduced the 32-bit, EISA bus, which accommodates the Pentium chip. EISA became fairly popular in the PC market.

- The PCI is a 32-bit local bus slot developed by Intel. Because they talk to the motherboard at 33 MHz, the PCI bus slots offer a significant improvement over ISA or EISA expansion slots. With the PCI bus, each add-on card contains information that the processor uses to automatically configure the card. The PCI bus is one of the three components necessary for Plug and Play. The main purpose of the PCI bus is to allow direct access to the CPU for devices such as memory and video. PCI expansion slots are the most common type in motherboards today.

- The AGP was developed by Intel. AGP is a dedicated high-speed bus that supports the high demands of graphical software. This slot is reserved for video adapters. It is the standard graphics port in all new systems. On AGP-equipped motherboards, a single AGP slot holds the display adapter, and another device can use the PCI slot. Slightly shorter than the white PCI slot, the AGP slot is usually a different color and is located about an inch beyond the PCI slot. AGP 2.0 currently defines an interface supporting 1x and 2x speeds at 3.3 V and 1x, 2x, and 4x speeds at 1.5 V signaling. AGP 3.0 is the latest specification defining the new signaling scheme for 4x and 8x speeds at .8 V signaling levels. AGP 3.0 delivers over 2.1 GBps of bandwidth to support graphic-intensive applications, including digital photos and video. Table 2-7 contains a summary of the different AGP modes with clock rate (approximate) and transfer rate.

Table 2-7 AGP Modes

Mode	Approximate Clock Rate (MHz)	Transfer Rate (MBps)
AGP 1X	66	266
AGP 2X	133	533
AGP 4X	266	1066
AGP 8X	533	2133

Riser Cards

You use a riser card, shown in Figure 2-10, when a computer is fully loaded. It physically extends a slot so you can plug in a chip or card. In low-profile, space-saving cases, cards are plugged into riser cards that reside parallel with the motherboard.

Figure 2-10 Riser Card

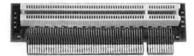

Figure 2-11 shows an Audio/Modem Riser (AMR), a plug-in card for an Intel motherboard. It contains audio or modem circuits. Intel specifies a 46-pin edge connector to provide the digital interface between the card and the motherboard. The AMR contains all the analog functions (codecs) required for audio and modem operation.

Figure 2-11 AMR Card

The AMR evolved into the Communications and Networking Riser (CNR) card, shown in Figure 2-12, which added LAN and home networking functions. The CNR is a 30-pin interface that accommodates two formats, making various audio/modem and audio/network combinations possible.

Figure 2-12 CNR Card

The Mobile Daughter Card (MDC) is the equivalent of the AMR for laptop computers.

Monitors and Display Devices

Computers are usually connected to a display device, also called a *monitor*. Figure 2-13 shows a monitor. Monitors are available in different types, sizes, and characteristics. When purchasing a new computer, you might have to purchase the monitor separately.

Figure 2-13 Computer Monitor

Understanding the characteristics of a good monitor helps you determine which type is best suited for a specific system. The following terms relate to monitors:

- **Pixels**—Picture elements. The screen image consists of pixels, or tiny dots. The pixels are arranged in rows across the screen. Each pixel consists of three colors, red, green, and blue (RGB). Examine the screen closely to see them.

- **Dot pitch**—A measurement of how close together the phosphor dots are on the screen. The finer the dot pitch, the better the image quality. Look for the smaller number. Most monitors today have a 0.25 mm dot pitch. Some have a 0.22 mm dot pitch, which gives a very fine resolution.

- **Refresh rate**—The rate at which the screen image is refreshed. Refresh rates are measured in hertz (Hz), which means times per second. The higher the refresh rate, the more steady the screen image. It might look like a steady picture, but actually the screen flickers every time the electron beam hits the phosphor-coated dots. Refresh rate is also called vertical frequency or vertical refresh rate.

- **Color depth**—The number of different colors each pixel can display. It is measured in bits. The higher the depth, the more colors the screen can produce.

- **Video RAM (VRAM)**—The memory a video card has. The more VRAM the video card has, the more colors it can display. The video card also sends out the refresh signal, thus controlling the refresh rate.

- **Resolution**—Varies based on the number of pixels. The more pixels in the screen, the better the resolution. Better resolution means a sharper image. The lowest screen resolution on modern PCs is 640 x 480 pixels, which is called Video Graphics Array (VGA). Super Video Graphics Array (SVGA) and Extended Graphics Array (XGA) have resolutions all the way up to 1600 x 1200 (see Table 2-8).

Table 2-8 Monitor Characteristics by Type

Standard	Resolution (Pixels)	Number of Pixels	Screen Size (Inches)	Refresh Rate (Hertz)
VGA	640 x 480	307,200	14	60–72 Hz
SVGA	800 x 600	480,000	15, 17	75–85 Hz
SVGA	1024 x 728	786,432	17, 19	75–85 Hz
XGA	1152 x 864	995,328	17, 19, 21	75–85 Hz
XGA	1280 x 1024	1,310,720	19, 21	75–85 Hz
XGA	1600 x 1200	1,920,000	21	75–85 Hz

- **Monitor screen sizes**—Measured in inches. The most common sizes are 14", 15", 17", 19", and 21" screens, measured diagonally. Note that the visible size is actually smaller than the measurement. Keep this note in mind when shopping for a monitor.
- **Display colors**—The colors are created by varying the light intensity of the three basic colors. The 24- and 32-bit colors are the usual choices for graphic artists and professional photographers. For most other applications, 16-bit color is sufficient. The following is a summary of the most common color depths:
  — 256 colors—8-bit color
  — 65,536 colors—16-bit color, also called 65K or HiColor
  — 16 million colors—24-bit color, also called True Color
  — 4 billion colors—32-bit color, also called True Color

A high-quality monitor and a high-quality video card are necessary for both a high resolution and a high refresh rate.

DVD Formats and Drives

A DVD is a type of optical disc that uses the same 120 mm diameter as a CD. The DVD looks like a CD, but the storage capacity is significantly higher. DVDs can be recorded on both sides, and some commercial versions can support two layers per side. This layering can provide more than 25 times the storage that CDs do.

DVD originally stood for Digital Video Disc. As the technology evolved in the computer world, the "video" portion was dropped. The DVD Forum (http://www.dvdforum.org) was founded in 1995 for the purpose of exchanging and disseminating ideas and information about the DVD Format and its technical capabilities, improvements, and innovations. The DVD Forum started using the term Digital Versatile Disc. Currently, both Digital Versatile Disk and Digital Video Disk are acceptable.

DVD Media

There are two types of media developed for DVDs, "plus" and "minus." The DVD Forum supports DVD media with a hyphen, such as DVD-R and DVD-RW. This media is called "minus R" or "minus RW." The DVD +RW Alliance was created in 1997 (http://www.dvdrw.com). The DVD +RW Alliance developed the plus standards, which include DVD+R and DVD+RW. The plus and minus were confusing until recently. In 2002, drives were introduced that support both the plus and minus types of media. Table 2-9 describes the types of DVD media and the sides, layers, and capacity.

Table 2-9 DVD Media by Type

Type	Sides	Layers	Capacity
Read Only			
DVD-Video	1	1	4.7 GB (DVD-5)
DVD-Video	1	2	8.5 GB (DVD-9)
DVD-ROM	2	1	9.4 GB (DVD-10)
DVD-ROM	2	2	17.0 GB (DVD-18)
Rewritable (100,000 Cycles)			
DVD-RAM Version 1	1	1	2.6 GB
DVD-RAM Version 1	2	1	5.2 GB
DVD-RAM Version 2	1	1	4.7 GB
DVD-RAM Version 2	2	1	9.4 GB
DVD-RAM (80 mm)	1	1	1.46 GB
DVD-RAM (80 mm)	2	1	2.92 GB
Re-Recordable (1000 Cycles)			
DVD-RW	1	1	4.7 GB
DVD+RW	1	1	4.7 GB
DVD+RW	2	1	9.4 GB

DVD Drives

As the price of DVD recordable and rewritable drives, shown in Figure 2-14, decreases, more computer systems will contain the drives. Currently, DVD players and combo drives are affordable and included in many computers. Combo drives are CD and DVD players together.

Figure 2-14 DVD Drive

How a DVD-ROM Works

As a CD does, a DVD stores data in the form of indentations and bumps on the reflective surface. The indentations are called *pits*, and the bumps are called *lands*.

When data is read, light from the laser bounces off the pits. The lands are located on the underside of the disk. The pits reflect less light, so they are read by the DVD drive as 0s. The lands reflect more light, so they are read as 1s. Together, these 1s and 0s make up the binary language understood by computers.

Speed, Access Time, and Transfer Rate

One specification for a DVD drive is its speed. The faster the disc spins, the faster it can transfer the data to computer memory. The DVD speed is indicated by a number with an "x" after it. For example, a 12-speed DVD is labeled 12x. The larger the number, the faster the disc can spin.

Two other important specifications to consider are the access time and data transfer rate. *Access time* is how quickly the drive can locate the data the user is looking for and position the laser. *Data transfer rate* is how fast the computer can transfer the information into memory.

DVD speed ratings for external drives will vary. Check the manufacturer's documentation for more information.

Other specifications that directly or indirectly influence speed, access time, or transfer rate are seek time, cache memory, interface type, and error correction.

Backup Hardware

To perform a backup (copying data and software), some backup hardware must be available on the network server. The most common backup hardware device (historically and now) is some form of magnetic tape drive. You can use other backup hardware devices for backup operations, but they are less common than tape drives.

A backup hardware device is a required part of any network server installation. Backup hardware devices can be expensive to purchase. However, the consequences of not having a backup hardware device on a network server, and thus not having a backup copy of the data and software, can be far more expensive.

Tape Drives

Tape drives are the most common devices for backing up data on a network server's disk drives. Tape devices are known for their long-lasting performance, which is partly due to the tape-drive mechanics that some systems include. A variety of tape devices use different tape formats for storing data. Many tape drives can also compress the data before it is stored on tape. In most cases, the compression ratio is 2:1. This compression has the effect of doubling the storage capacity of the tape.

Quarter Inch Cartridge

3M created the *Quarter Inch Cartridge* (QIC, pronounced "quick") in 1972 as a tape standard. As the name implies, the tape in QIC is one-quarter–inch wide. There have been many versions of the QIC tape drives over the years. Table 2-10 summarizes QIC standards. Early QIC tape drives actually attached to the floppy-disk controller in the computer. Later versions could be attached to the parallel port on the computer. Still later versions used the IDE hard-disk drive interface. The QIC standard has limited storage capacity and appears only in entry-level network servers.

Table 2-10 QIC Tape Standards

QIC Standards	QIC Cartridge	Storage Capacity (Native/Compressed)	Interface
QIC-40	DC-2000	40 MB/80 MB	Floppy
QIC-40	DC-2060	60 MB/120 MB	Floppy
QIC-80	MC-2120	125 MB/250 MB	Floppy, parallel
QIC-80	MC-2120Extra	400 MB/800 MB	Floppy, parallel
QIC-80XL	MC-2120XL	170 MB/340 MB	Floppy, parallel
QIC-3020XL	MC-3020X1	680 MB/1.36 GB	Floppy, parallel, IDE
QIC-3020XL	MC-3020Extra	1.6 GB/3.2 GB	Floppy, parallel, IDE
QIC-3095	MC-3095	4 GB/8 GB	IDE, SCSI-2
QIC-3220	MC-3220	10 GB/20 GB	SCSI-2
QIC-5010	DC-5010	16 GB/32 GB	SCSI-2
QIC-5210	DC-5210	25 GB/50 GB	SCSI-2

Travan Cartridge Tape

A 3M spin-off (Imation) company introduced the Travan cartridge tape standard in 1994.
Table 2-11 summarizes the Travan tape standards. Travan is based on QIC technology and in
many cases is either read- and write-compatible with some QIC tape cartridges or read-com-
patible with QIC cartridges. Travan tape drives have a higher storage capacity than the older
QIC tape drives. Travan's most recent standard was hardware compression. It would free a
server's processor, allowing the processor to execute other tasks at the same time. Travan tape
drives have the capacity to back up low-end network servers but are relatively slow. Backup
speed is about 1 MBps.

Table 2-11 Travan Tape Standards

Travan Standards	Tape Cartridge	Storage Capacity (Native/Compressed)	Interface
Travan-1	TR-1	400 MB/800 MB	Floppy, parallel
Travan-2	TR-2	800 MB/1.6 GB	Floppy, parallel
Travan-3	TR-3	1.6 GB/3.2 GB	Floppy, parallel
Travan-4	TR-4	4 GB/8 GB	SCSI-2, EIDE
Travan NS-8	TR-8	4 GB/8 GB	SCSI-2, EIDE
Travan-5	TR-5	10 GB/20 GB	SCSI-2, EIDE
Travan NS-20	TR-20	10 GB/20 GB	SCSI-2, EIDE

8 mm Tape

Exabyte Corporation pioneered tape technology that uses the 8 mm tape. The technology uses a
tape similar to 8 mm videotape and the same helical scan system used by a VCR. Table 2-12
reviews 8 mm tape technologies.

Table 2-12 8 mm Tape Technologies

8 mm Tape Technology	Storage Capacity (Native/Compressed)	Transfer Speed
8200	2.5 GB/5 GB	246 KBps
8500	5 GB/10 GB	500 KBps

Mammoth 8 mm tape technologies are an improvement on the original 8 mm tape technologies
with higher storage capacities and faster transfer speeds. Table 2-13 reviews Mammoth 8 mm
tape technologies.

Table 2-13 Mammoth 8 mm Tape Technologies

Mammoth Technology	Storage Capacity (Native/Compressed)	Transfer Speed
Mammoth-1	20 GB/40 GB	3 MBps
Mammoth-2	60 GB/120 GB	12 MBps

Advanced Intelligent Tape

Advanced Intelligent Tape (AIT) technology was originally developed by Sony and introduced in 1996. AIT technology uses 8 mm tapes that use the helical scan recording hardware (much like a VCR). AIT tapes actually have memory in the tape cartridge, known as *Memory-In-Cassette (MIC),* which stores the tape log to facilitate locating a file during a restore operation. Table 2-14 summarizes AIT tape standards. For more information about AIT technology, see the AIT Forum website at http://www.aittape.com.

Table 2-14 AIT Tape Standards

AIT Standard	Tape Medium	Storage Capacity (Native/Compressed	Transfer Speed
AIT-1	SDX125C	25 GB/50 GB	3 MBps
AIT-1	SDX135C	35 GB/70 GB	3 MBps
AIT-2	SDX236C	36 GB/72 GB	6 MBps
AIT-2	SDX250C	50 GB/100 GB	6 MBps
AIT-3	Prototype	100 GB/200 GB	12 MBps

Digital Audio Tape

The *Digital Audio Tape (DAT)* tape standard uses 4 mm digital audiotapes to store data in the *Digital Data Storage (DSS)* format. There are currently four different DDS standards. Table 2-15 summarizes DAT standards.

Table 2-15 DAT Tape Standards

DDS Standard	Storage Capacity (Native/Compressed)	Transfer Speed	Also Known As
DDS-1	2 GB/4 GB	1 MBps	–
DDS-2	4 GB/8 GB	1 MBps	DAT8
DDS-3	12 GB/24 GB	2 MBps	DAT24
DDS-4	20 GB/40 GB	6 MBps	DAT40

Digital Linear Tape

Digital Linear Tape (DLT) technology offers high-capacity and relatively high-speed tape backup capabilities. DLT tapes record information on the tape in a linear format, unlike 8 mm tape technologies that use helical scan recording techniques. DLT tape drives support a high storage capacity along with a fast transfer speed; depending on the media, it allows up to 70 GB of compressed data. However, DLT tape drives are expensive. Table 2-16 compares DLT formats.

Table 2-16 DLT Tape Formats

DLT Standard	Storage Capacity (Native/Compressed)	Transfer Speed
DLT-2000	10 GB/20 GB	1.25 MBps
DLT-2000XT	15 GB/30 GB	1.25 MBps
DLT-4000	20 GB/40 GB	1.5 MBps
DLT-7000	35 GB/70 GB	5 MBps
DLT-8000	40 GB/80 GB	6 MBps
Super DLT	110 GB/220 GB	11 MBps

Linear Tape-Open

Hewlett-Packard, IBM, and Seagate developed the *Linear Tape-Open (LTO)* technology. LTO comes in two distinct forms: one designed for high storage capacity (Ultrium) and one designed for fast access (Accelis). Table 2-17 reviews the LTO tape formats. For more information about LTO tape technology, see the LTO website at http://www.lto-technology.com.

Table 2-17 LTO Tape Formats

LTO Format	Storage Capacity (Native/Compressed)	Transfer Speed (Native/Compressed)
Ultrium	100 GB/200 GB	20 MBps/40 Mbps
Accelis	25 GB/50 GB	20 MBps/40 Mbps

Tape Arrays

Several network server vendors offer an array of tape drives with fault-tolerance characteristics. Most of these technologies use four identical tape drives and implement the tape version of RAID, which is called *Redundant Array of Independent Tapes (RAIT)*. You can use RAIT for mirroring tape drives or implement it (with at least three tape drives) as data striping with parity. The result is that if a tape is damaged or lost, data recovery can still occur.

Tape Autochangers

A *tape autochanger* (also known as a *tape auto loade*r) allows the tape drive to load a new tape when the current tape gets full while performing a backup. This automation relieves the operator from having to remove one tape and insert a new tape. It is handy because backups are usually performed in the dead of night. Most tape autochangers support unloading and loading a limited number of tapes (10 or fewer).

Tape Libraries

A *tape library* is usually an external system that has multiple tape drives; tens or hundreds of tapes; and an automatic mechanism for locating the tapes, loading them into the tape drives, and returning the tapes to the proper location. With all this intelligence and sophistication, it should be obvious that tape libraries are the high end of backup systems (which means that they are expensive).

USB Flash Memory

USB flash memory, shown in Figure 2-15, is a relatively new type of storage device. It can hold hundreds of times the data that a floppy disk can. They are available to store 16 MB, 32 MB, 64 MB, 128 MB, 256 MB, 512 MB, and 1 GB. USB 1.1 is capable of read speeds of up to 1 MBps and write speeds of up to 900 KBps. The latest version is USB 2.0. It is capable of read speeds of up to 6 MBps and write speeds of up to 4.5 MBps.

Figure 2-15 USB Flash Memory

Portable Devices

Notebook Computers

Portable devices incorporate the system unit, input unit, and output unit into a single, lightweight package. A user can carry portable devices around, unlike towers or desktops. These devices are also called notebook computers, laptop computers, palmtops, or PDAs, depending on their size and function. The focus in this section is notebook and laptop computers, but the issues discussed are common to all portables.

Producing portable computers has not been problem-free. Early attempts at developing a portable computer produced heavy systems with short operating times between battery recharges. Advancements in technology, particularly in integrated circuits (IC) and peripheral component designs, produced a portable that competes with desktop and tower systems in speed, power, and number of features. A typical notebook computer, such as the one depicted in Figure 2-16, has many features:

- A video display that is larger than those typically associated with the older PC-AT machines
- A hard drive with a capacity in the tens of gigabytes
- CD-ROM/DVD drives

Figure 2-16 Notebook Computer

Using a notebook computer is different from using a desktop in several ways. The built-in keyboard on a notebook is smaller than the keyboard for a desktop. To keep it compact, notebooks do not have a separate mouse but instead use one of the following input devices:

- **Trackball**—Shown in Figure 2–17, this rotating ball allows the cursor to move on the screen.
- **Trackpoint**—Shown in Figure 2–18, the trackpoint moves the cursor when you push a finger over the point.
- **Touchpad**—Shown in Figure 2–19, the touchpad moves the cursor when you slide a finger across the pad. You can scroll and even click to open programs.

As technology improves, notebook components are using less power but are becoming more rugged. These concepts are explored further in the sections that follow.

Figure 2-17 Trackball Mouse

Figure 2-18 Trackpoint

Figure 2-19 Touchpad

Portable Hardware

Portable computers are built to be lightweight and to fit a certain size or form factor. These goals have led to special considerations in developing the hardware components for portables. This section explores some of these components.

Power Sources

Notebook computers typically come equipped with an AC-to-DC power adapter. In addition, auto adapters let you use the notebook and recharge the batteries in a car. These adapters are proprietary, so availability depends on the specific manufacturer. Notebooks and other portable devices are built to be used anywhere, even where power outlets are not available. To solve this problem, batteries are an integrated component of portable systems.

Originally, portables used Nickel Cadmium (Ni-Cad) batteries, as shown in Figure 2-20. These batteries were in an external battery pack attached to the portable device. The average amount of time Ni-Cad batteries would operate a device was only 30 to 45 minutes when first introduced, depending on power consumption. The time to operate increased to 45 to 75 minutes, depending on the screen size and the application that was open. In addition, the time to recharge these batteries could be nearly a day. Better batteries now address these limitations.

Figure 2-20 Ni-Cad Batteries

More recently, portables use Nickel Metal-Hydride (NiMH) and Lithium-Ion batteries, shown in Figure 2-21. These batteries are usually constructed in a plastic holder that you can easily insert into the portable device. These batteries usually last for just over two hours, depending on their size and the power consumption of the device. It takes only three to five hours to recharge them.

Figure 2-21 Lithium-Ion Batteries

One drawback to portable systems is that there are currently no industry standards in place for the power supplies. Therefore, a battery in one portable device might not be compatible with a different portable device.

Many notebook computers have power-management software to extend the battery life or conserve battery power when the battery is low. When a notebook battery gets low, it starts to run more slowly. The internal power-management software monitors how the notebook is being used. It indicates that the power supply is running low, providing time to save any work. When you receive this warning, plug in the computer AC adapter or quit and recharge the battery.

Hard Drives

As with most components of a portable device, hard drives have been specially developed to be smaller and use less power to accommodate size and power limitations. The size of hard drives in portable devices ranges dramatically. A portable hard drive powers down to save power if it has not been accessed for a certain period of time.

Storage Devices and Removable Storage

Current notebooks have not only adequate hard drive storage, but also CD-RW and floppy drives. To make the notebook smaller, some manufacturers provide for an external CD-ROM and floppy disk drive. Because notebooks typically have a USB port, they can also take advantage of the new USB storage units.

PCMCIA Cards

The Personal Computer Memory Card International Association (PCMCIA) card was introduced in 1989. The PCMCIA is a special expansion card designed primarily to accommodate the needs of the portable-computer market. You can use these cards to upgrade a notebook by adding memory, a modem, a network connection, or a peripheral device. Recently, the term PCMCIA has been replaced by *PC Card*. There are three types of PCMCIA slots and cards, as shown in Figure 2-22:

- Type I cards are 3.3 mm thick and used as memory expansion units.
- Type II cards are 5 mm thick and used for any expansion device except hard drives.
- Type III cards are 10.5 mm thick and designed solely for hard drives.

Figure 2-22 PCMCIA Card Types

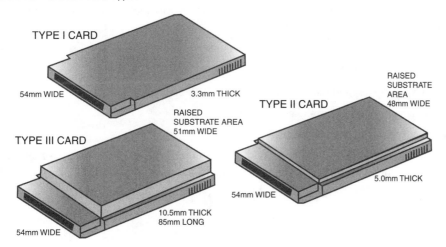

The newer Mini PCI card is used primarily for notebooks, web pads, Internet appliances, and other mobile data applications:

- Type I Mini PCI cards are designed for flexibility in placement of the card by using cabling to connect to the I/O. They are used primarily in full-featured systems, typically for desktop replacements.
- Type II cards are designed for value-priced systems with on-board modular connectors. Type II is the simplest to maintain and warranty.
- Type III cards are designed for the thin systems, which are becoming increasingly prevalent in the high-end notebook segment.

Memory

The standard Small Outline Dual Inline Memory Module (SODIMM) is used most often in notebook computers. Some notebooks use the proprietary memory modules of the manufacturer. At least 64 MB of RAM is recommended as sufficient memory for the operating system and application software. Check the user documentation for information on upgrading notebook memory. Some notebooks are equipped with access panels that makes it easy to plug in additional memory chips.

Most portable computers do not use a standard type of memory. With nearly any notebook, you need to seek out the manufacturer website or user manual for more information about upgrading memory. Memory types can vary between different products or different versions of the same product. You must research before upgrading the memory in a portable.

Portable Computer Displays

Because of the compact nature and limited power supply of notebook computers and other portables, they use non-cathode–ray tube (CRT) displays. Two examples of such displays are Liquid Crystal Display (LCD) and gas-plasma panels. These two types of display systems are suited to the portability needs of portable computers for a number of reasons:

- They are lighter and more compact than CRT monitors.
- They require less electrical energy to operate.
- They can be operated from batteries.

LCDs are the flat-panel displays in most of the newer portable systems. They have the advantage of being thin, flat, and lightweight, and they require little power to operate. Additionally, these displays offer better reliability and longer life than CRT units. Figure 2-23 shows an LCD display on a PDA.

Figure 2-23 LCD Display

NOTE

Portable display panels are powered by low-voltage DC power sources such as a battery or converter. The CRT displays are commonly plugged directly to the wall AC outlet.

Docking Stations and Port Replicators

A docking station, shown in Figure 2-24, allows the portable PC to operate with hardware devices associated with desktop computers. A docking station is also called a *docking port*. You insert a notebook into the docking station. Then, the extension bus in the docking station plugs into the expansion connector in the notebook. Usually, a docking station provides standard PC expansion slots. Therefore, you can use non-notebook peripheral devices, such as network adapters, sound cards, and so on, with the system. When a notebook computer is in a docking station, its normal I/O devices are disabled, and the docking station peripherals take over. This setup makes it possible for the notebook to use a collection of desktop devices that are otherwise not available to it. Desktop devices include an AC power source, CRT monitor, full-sized keyboard, mouse, modem, and standard PC port connectors.

The notebook and the docking station communicate with each other through a special docking port connector in the rear of the notebook. However, most docking stations are proprietary. You can only use them with the portables they were designed to work with. The proprietary nature of these products come from two factors:

- The connector in the notebook must correctly align with the docking port connection in the docking station.
- The notebook unit must fit correctly within the docking station opening.

Currently, there are no standards for portable systems. Therefore, there is little chance that two different manufacturers would locate the connectors in the same places or design the same case outline.

A port replicator, shown in Figure 2-25, serves a similar purpose as a docking station. It is a device that connects multiple peripherals to a notebook. The difference is that the port replicator does not contain any slots for expansion, speakers, or peripherals. The desktop devices are permanently plugged into the port replicator. The port replicator connects to the notebook via a large plug and socket that duplicates all the cable lines for the monitor, printer, keyboard, and mouse.

Figure 2-24 HP Omnibook Docking Station

Figure 2-25 Port Replicator

Upgrading Notebooks

Currently, you can upgrade most components in notebook computers to provide for more memory, faster processing, increased storage, and faster Internet connections. Because notebook computers are proprietary, it is important to verify the components are upgradeable. The best source is user documentation or the manufacturer website.

Troubleshooting Notebooks

Like their desktop counterparts, notebooks need regular maintenance. Using the system tools on a weekly basis will keep the system running smoothly. System tools are covered thoroughly in Chapter 11, "Preventive Maintenance."

A common problem for notebook computers is overheating. Overheating can cause the system to slow down and malfunction. When the notebook restarts without any notice, it might be a sign that the notebook is overheating. Keeping the notebook cooler can be as simple as raising the notebook slightly to allow air to circulate under the computer. There are inexpensive devices that can achieve this effect. Also, you can purchase notebook cooler pads that utilize fans powered by the USB port to keep the notebook cool.

Infrared Devices

An infrared port allows infrared devices to communicate with each other. Figure 2-26 shows the receiving port. Infrared technology, also known as Infrared Radiation (IR), is used for wireless transmission between computer devices and in remote controls for television and stereo systems. All specifications use bidirectional communication. The frequencies of IR are higher than those of microwaves but lower than those of visible light. To successfully link two devices, you must have a transmitter and a receiver with an unobstructed line of sight between the devices. Usually, you set the computer device, such as a PDA or laptop, close to the device for communication (such as a printer), but you can use distances up to 2.5 ft.

Figure 2-26 Infrared Devices

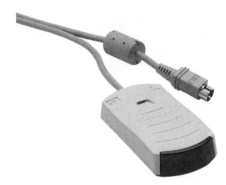

Wireless Access Points

Wireless networking technologies allow computers to broadcast their information to one another using radio signals. Computers in a client/server network communicate through a wireless access point, shown in Figure 2-27. This wired controller receives and transmits data to the wireless adapters installed on each system. Installing a wireless adapter on a notebook computer, as shown in Figure 2-28, allows the computer to work anywhere within range of the wireless access point.

Figure 2-27 Wireless Access Points

Figure 2-28 Wireless Adapter

Chapter 3

Assembling a Computer

Desktops

The desktop design shown in Figure 3-1 is one of the more familiar case styles. Desktop units are designed to sit horizontally on the desktop. The first IBM computers, the original IBM-PC, XT, and AT designs, use this case style. The two sizes of most desktop cases are slim-line and regular.

Figure 3-1 Desktop Computer Case

You must consider two important characteristics when choosing a desktop case style for a computer.

Available desktop space is important when the computer has to share the desktop with the monitor and other peripherals. Avoid buying the slim-line unit because it is small, it has little room for expansion, and it is designed for business environments.

The form factor is another characteristic to consider. The form factor describes the general layout of the computer case, the positioning of the slots in the case, and the type of motherboard the case will accommodate. The newest form factor, and the one most often encountered, is the ATX. The ATX form factor is designed for better airflow and easier access to the common components.

Towers

Tower cases are usually designed to sit vertically on the floor beneath a desk. To provide more usable workspace on the desktop, some users in the past resorted to standing the desktop cases on their sides under desks. Computer makers then developed cases that would naturally fit under the desk. In general, tower cases have enough bays to hold floppy drives, CD-ROM drives, tape drives, DVD drives, and anything else that you might install. The internal design of a tower system resembles that of the desktop unit. Tower cases come in three sizes:

- Mini towers
- Mid towers
- Full-size towers

Shown in Figures 3-2 and 3-3, mini towers and mid towers are shorter and less expensive than their full-size counterparts, shown in Figure 3-4. The one major drawback when choosing the smaller tower is that it does not have enough room for internal add-ons or disk drives.

NOTE

You can add external devices to mini- and mid-tower computers if there is insufficient room inside the case for an internal device. Typically, these external devices cost slightly more and use external ports.

Figure 3-2 Mini Tower

Figure 3-3 Mid Tower

Figure 3-4 Full-Size Tower

Many easy-access schemes allow quick or convenient access to the inside of the system case. Some towers, for example, use removable trays that let you plug in the motherboard and I/O cards before sliding them into the unit. Other tower cases use hinged doors on the side of the case, allowing the system and I/O boards to swing away from the chassis. Either of these features facilitates the process of assembling the computer.

It is important to note that the ventilation of some tower units tends to be poor because the I/O cards are mounted horizontally. When the heat generated by the boards rises, it passes the upper boards, which are then subjected to additional heat. Most tower cases include a secondary case fan to help increase the airflow and dissipate excessive heat.

Installing Floppy Disk Drives

The step-by-step process for installing the floppy drive is fairly simple. Make sure that the floppy cables and power cables are long enough to reach the drive before starting. Also verify that the drive is mounted right-side up or it will not work. Figure 3-5 shows a floppy-disk drive. Use the following steps to install either a 3.5" or 5.25" drive:

Step 1   Select which drive bay you will use for the floppy drive, either a 3.5" bay or a 5.25" bay. Remove the faceplate of that bay. Save the faceplate for future use. To mount a 3.5" drive into a 5.25" bay, you might need a special bracket that usually comes with the new floppy drive.

Step 2   Without connecting anything yet, insert the drive into the chosen bay, making sure it fits properly.

Step 3   Select the right-size screws if you don't use those that came with the drive. If you are using brackets to hold the drive in place, secure them now, or simply use the screws to attach the drive to the bay. First, tighten the screws by hand, and then use a screwdriver to secure the screws. Make sure they are not too tight, and take care not to cross thread or strip the screws.

Step 4   Attach the power and ribbon cable to the drive. If you are going to install other drives, you can skip this step. Attaching these items provides more maneuvering room in the case, especially if there are no removable drive bays. You can connect the drive cable and power cord after you install all the drives.

Step 5   Check your work.

Figure 3-5 Floppy-Disk Drive

NOTE

Know what makes a floppy drive A or B and how to set up the drives to function as either master or slave.

Attaching the Hard Drive and CD-ROM or DVD-ROM

This section describes how to attach both the hard drive and CD-ROM to the case processes.

Before proceeding, make sure that the interface cable will reach the drive in its intended location. With IDE and ATA drives, the length of the cable is limited to 18" or less, in some cases. Also, make sure that the power cable will reach the drive from the power supply. Do not mount the drive upside down or backwards. Verify the label of the drive is up and the circuit board is down.

The first step to attaching the hard drive is setting the jumpers. See the sidebar, "Master and Slave Jumper Settings" for information on how to do this.

Master and Slave Jumper Settings
The designation of a hard drive or CD-ROM drive as either master or slave is generally determined by the jumper configuration. The only exception is if the drive is set to "cable select" and both the system and ribbon cable support cable select. In this case, master and slave are determined by the position on the data ribbon cable. Depending on how the system controls the cable, the select line on the ribbon cable determines where you need to attach the master and slave. Refer to the system manual for more information. This description applies only to a situation where both drives are attached to the same IDE channel, where the CD-ROM is set to slave. For better performance, always attach the drives to separate channels. The hard drive should be attached to the primary IDE channel as primary master and the CD-ROM to the second IDE channel as secondary master.

Master and Slave Jumper Settings (Continued)

It is easier to configure these drives before installing them in the computer case because you will have more room to set the jumpers. Before setting the jumpers, determine the types and number of drives to install. It is assumed here that there are two IDE drives. The jumper settings are often printed on top of the drive itself. If not, consult the manual. In either case, use needle-nosed pliers or tweezers to set the jumpers. Always save spare jumpers for future use by hanging them on one pin.

Hanging the jumper on one pin is the same as not jumpering; that is, you have selected no circuit configuration. This move is also known as "parking" a jumper. Figure 3-6 illustrates some typical jumper settings on an IDE drive.

Figure 3-6 Jumper Settings on an IDE Drive

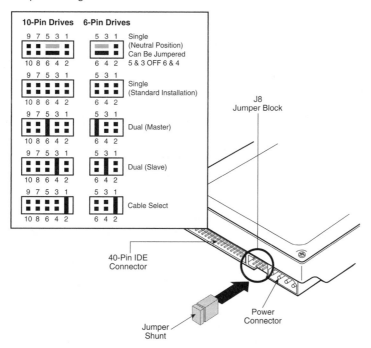

In a basic system that only has one hard drive, set the jumper to master. Some drives have another setting called *single*. This setting essentially tells the drive that it is alone on that IDE channel and it works the same as the master. It is recommended to use this setting, if available, on a system with one hard drive. The CD-ROM is also easy to configure. However, jumpers might be located in different places on each drive and might even be labeled differently. Set the CD-ROM to master if it is the only drive connected to the second IDE channel.

Technically, you can insert the hard drive into any free bay in a computer case. However, consider the following issues:

- Hard drives, especially the newer 7200 RPM and 10,000 RPM drives, can generate a lot of heat. Keep these drives as far away from other hardware as possible.
- If it is necessary to install a drive cooler, make sure that there is enough room.

- Install a hard drive away from the power supply. Poorly designed cases might give room under the power supply to install the hard drive, but that is not a good place for a hard drive. Power supplies act like magnets and can damage data.
- Finally, keep the hard drive near the front of the case. It will benefit from the cooling effect of the air current drawn into the case through the front by the system cooling fans.

With the previous considerations in mind, use the following steps when mounting a hard drive:

Step 1   Set the hard-drive jumper to master, as previously explained.

Step 2   Slide the drive into the selected drive rail of the case. Recall that you do not need to remove the faceplate in this area. Modern ATX cases usually provide a hard-drive bay without a faceplate. If the drive is smaller than the bay, add rails or a mounting bracket to make it fit.

Step 3   Select the right-size screws if you don't use those packaged with the drive. Screw the drive into place, making sure not to force anything. Tighten the screws by hand first and then tighten them with a screwdriver.

Step 4   Attach the ribbon cable and the power cord to the hard drive, the same way as with the floppy drive. Normally, the ribbon cable goes from the primary controller of the motherboard to the drive.

NOTE

Do not tighten the screws until you connect the cables to the drive.

Now, you need to attach the CD-ROM and DVD. CD-ROM and DVD player installation is similar to hard-drive installation. For the CD-ROM, remove the drive-bay cover first. Then, set the CD-ROM jumper to master because it will be connected to the secondary IDE channel. Now, slide the drive into the bay from the front, making sure that it is flush with the front panel, and screw it in place. Use the same procedure when installing a DVD player.

In some computer cases, particularly the mini towers, it can be challenging to work behind the CD-ROM because of its length and because it is obstructed by the power supply.

The Role of Drive Rails

As with the hard drive, the physical installation of the CD-ROM and DVD depends on the case design or type. Some cases come with drive rails to help install hardware. Simply screw a drive rail in the correct direction to each side of the CD-ROM. Then, slide the CD-ROM into the computer case from the front, using the rails as a guide until it snaps into place. Use the same procedure to install a DVD player. Drive rails make hardware installations relatively easy.

Connecting the Floppy Drive, Hard Drive, CD-ROM and DVD

The floppy drive, hard drive, CD-ROM, and DVD player communicate with the rest of the system using ribbon cables. This section discusses the types of ribbon cables as well as how to connect them to the various drives.

Connecting the Floppy Drive

The following steps detail how to connect the floppy drive to the motherboard:

Step 1   Identify the appropriate ribbon cable that goes with the floppy drive. It has a seven-wire twist toward one end and is smaller in width, 34-pins, compared to the 40-pin IDE ribbon cable.

Step 2   Identify Pin 1, the red edge of the cable, and align this with Pin 1 on the rear of the floppy drive. Gently push on the cable connector until it is fully inserted. In most cases, the connectors are keyed. If you experience any resistance as you attach the cable, then recheck the Pin 1 alignment. Because you are installing this drive as Drive A, be sure to use the connector past the twist in the cable.

Step 3   Now, identify the floppy controller on the system board by consulting the motherboard manual. Attach the connector on the far end of the ribbon cable to the floppy controller on the board. Make sure Pin 1 is properly aligned for the cable and controller interface connectors.

Step 4   Check your work at this point, making sure that no pin is bent or displaced.

If you accidentally reverse Pin 1, the drive will not work and the drive light will stay on until you correct it.

Connecting the Hard Drive, CD-ROM, and DVD

The following steps detail how to connect the hard drive, CD-ROM, and DVD player to the motherboard:

Step 1   Identify the two 40-pin IDE ribbon cables that go with the hard drive and CD-ROM. They are wider than the floppy cable and have no twist at one end.

Step 2   Attach one end of one cable connector to the rear of the hard-drive connector and one end of the second cable to the rear of the CD-ROM. You might have to slide the CD-ROM out a few inches to get enough access at the rear. Both cable connectors are keyed. Make sure that Pin 1 is properly aligned for the cable and drive connectors. The end of the cable with the longer span is usually connected to the motherboard.

Step 3   Now, attach the free end of the hard drive cable to IDE controller 1, the primary IDE, on the motherboard. Attach the free end of the CD-ROM cable to IDE controller 2, the secondary IDE, on the motherboard. Make sure Pin 1 on each cable is aligned with Pin 1 of the corresponding

NOTE

Pin 1 on both the hard drive and CD-ROM drive is usually located on the side closest to the power connector. Pin 1 might be labeled on the back of the hard drive. Conversely, Pin 1 on the motherboard might not be properly labeled, so consult your manual to make this determination. The CD-ROM drive audio cable can remain disconnected until you install a sound card.

controller interface. Installing the hard drive and CD-ROM on separate IDE channels can improve performance.

Step 4   Check your work, making sure all cable connectors are properly seated, no pins are displaced, and all Pin 1s are aligned.

If the hard-drive cable is backwards, you might get some strange errors that make the new drive appear as if it has "died" already. If you do, remove the hard-drive cable and reinstall.

Characterizing Ribbon Cables

Ribbon cables are widely used to connect peripherals such as floppy drives and hard drives internally. They are rarely used outside of the system case. They are thin, flat, multiconductor cables that you must connect correctly or the component will not work.

Floppy Drive Cable

The floppy drive exchanges data with the motherboard devices, including the microprocessor, via a 34-pin flat-ribbon cable. The ribbon cable typically connects from a 34-pin male connector at the rear of the floppy drive to a 34-pin male connector on the motherboard. The cable plugs, drive connector, and floppy controller interface are all keyed for proper alignment. Usually, a red stripe on the edge of the cable identifies Pin 1, as shown in Figure 3-7.

Figure 3-7 Pin 1 Ribbon Cable Identification

Lining the red-stripe edge with Pin 1 of the drive connector or drive-controller interface ensures correct alignment.

Current system BIOS versions can support up to two floppy drives on one controller through a daisy-chain cable arrangement. Cable pin-outs 10 through 16 are cross-wired between the middle drive connector and end drive connector. This wiring produces a twist that reverses the Drive Select (DS) configuration of the drive plugged into the end connector of the ribbon

CAUTION

Pin 1 on most floppy data connectors is usually on the near side to the power connector. However, floppy drives from different manufacturers can have their data connectors reversed so that Pin 1 and the red wire on the ribbon cable point away from the power connector. Also, some floppy-disk drives do not clearly mark Pin 1 on the data connector. In these cases, an incorrectly oriented cable becomes immediately apparent when you power up because the floppy-drive LED light comes on immediately and stays on.

cable. The twist consists of seven data wires. This feature, called *cable select*, automatically configures the drive on the middle connector as Drive B and the drive on the end connector as Drive A. This feature greatly simplifies the installation and configuration of floppy drives. This example uses only one 3.5" floppy, Drive A.

HDD and CD-ROM Cables

The hard drive, CD-ROM, and DVD player exchange data signals with the controller on the motherboard by means of a flat-ribbon cable, just like the floppy drive. The ribbon cable pin-outs and cable width depend on the type of interface. This course uses the IDE interface. The ribbon cable in this case looks physically similar to the floppy cable mentioned earlier, but it is wider, as shown in Figure 3-8. Pin 1 is also identified by a red edge. However, an IDE cable typically has 40 pins and can also have two devices attached to it, as with the floppy cable. In this case, however, you must set one device as the master and the other as a slave using jumpers. A second cable is called IDE 2, and it can have a master and a slave. The cable connectors and plugs, as with the floppy cable, are keyed for proper alignment.

Figure 3-8 Hard Drive Ribbon Cable

After becoming familiar with ribbon cables, you can connect these components to the system board.

Connecting Power Cables to the Floppy Drive, Hard Drive, CD-ROM, and DVD

Small cable drive connectors from the power supply provide power to the floppy drive, hard drive, CD-ROM, and DVD player. The cable connectors have a female 4-pin plug that connects to a male 4-pin connector at the rear of each drive. The pin-outs or wire scheme are color-coded so you can identify the proper voltages of the wires.

All the connectors are keyed and therefore can only be inserted one way, making it easy to attach the power cables to the drive. Verify that the proper connector is going to the appropriate drive, as described here:

- **Floppy drive**—Identify the proper connector that goes with the 3.5" drive. These connectors are usually the smallest plugs coming out of the power supply. Push the plugs in gently. Do not rock them back and forth to secure a connection.

- **Hard drive, CD-ROM, DVD**—Identify the proper power connectors for these drives. They are larger than those for the floppy, and sometimes the labels are P1, P2, P3, and so on. They are harder to push in, so rock them gently back and forth if needed until they snap into place.

As always, double-check all the work to make sure that all power plugs are properly inserted and secure.

The video on the CD-ROM included in the *Companion Guide*, "Installing the Floppy Drive, Hard Drive, and CD-ROM Drive," provides detailed steps for this installation process.

Power Voltage Requirements

You need two different power voltages for the proper functioning of these drives. The circuit board and the logic chips that each drive uses are designed to use +5 V power. The drive motors use +12 V power (see Table 3-1).

Table 3-18 Power Connector Pin-Outs

Pin No.	Signal	Wire Color
1	+5 V	Red
2	Ground	Black
3	Ground	Black
4	+12 V	Yellow

Chapter 6

Multimedia Capabilities

The Video Adapter

A *video adapter* (also called a display adapter or video board) is an integrated circuit card in a computer or, in some cases, a monitor that provides digital-to-analog conversion, video RAM, and a video controller so that data can be sent to a computer display. Figures 6-1 and 6-2 show the front of the video adapter and a side view.

Figure 6-1 Video Adapter—Front View

Figure 6-2 Video Adapter—Side View

Today, almost all displays and video adapters adhere to the standard Video Graphics Array (VGA). VGA outlines how data is passed between the computer and the display. It is responsible for the frame refresh rates in hertz and the number and width of horizontal lines, which essentially amount to specifying the resolution of the pixels that are created. VGA supports four different resolution settings and two related image refresh rates.

In addition to VGA, most displays adhere to one or more standards set by the Video Electronics Standards Association (VESA). The VESA defines how software can determine the capability of a display. It also identifies resolutions beyond those of VGA. These resolutions include 800 x 600, 1024 x 768, 1280 x 1024, and 1600 x 1200 pixels.

What Is a Display?

A display or monitor is a computer output surface and projecting mechanism that shows text and graphic images, using a cathode ray tube (CRT), liquid crystal display (LCD), light-emitting diode, gas plasma, or other image-projection technology. The display is usually considered to include the screen or projection surface and the device that produces the information on the screen. In some computers, the display is packaged in a separate unit called a monitor. Figure 6-3 shows a typical flat panel monitor. In other computers, the display is integrated into a unit with the processor and other parts of the computer. Some sources make the distinction that the monitor includes other signal-handling devices that feed and control the display or projection device. However, there is no distinction when all these parts are integrated into a total unit, as in the case of notebook computers. A video display terminal (VDT) or video display unit (VDU) typically refers to a terminal with a display and a keyboard.

Figure 6-3 Flat Panel Monitor

Most computer monitors use analog signals to display an image. This requirement and the need to continually refresh the displayed image mean that the computer also needs a display or video adapter. The video adapter takes the digital data sent by application programs, stores it in video random-access memory (video RAM), and converts it to analog data for the display scanning mechanism using a digital-to-analog converter (DAC).

Sound Cards and Speaker Systems

Typically, the output of the sound card requires additional amplification if the computer has external speakers. Figure 6-4 shows external speakers. The amplification circuitry is normally included in the external speaker units. Power for older speakers was derived from batteries housed in the speaker cabinets or from a small AC power converter. Most sound cards today have the capability of directly driving low-power headphones. The system's internal speaker can also produce audio output, or it can be amplified through external audio amplifier systems for applications such as Surround Sound.

Figure 6-4 External Computer Speakers

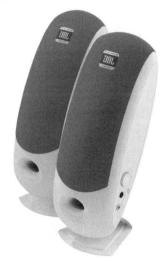

Digital Cameras and Video Cameras

A digital camera, shown in Figure 6-5, has a series of lenses that focus light to create an image of a scene, as does a conventional film camera. It focuses light onto a semiconductor device that records the light electronically instead of focusing this light onto a piece of film. It is this electronic information that is broken down into digital data by the computer. This step is what allows users to view, edit, e-mail, and post pictures to the Internet.

Figure 6-5 Digital Camera with Docking Station

A charge coupled device (CCD) is the image sensor used by most digital cameras. Some of the more inexpensive cameras use complementary metal oxide semiconductor (CMOS) technology. Although CMOS sensors are improving all the time, the CCD technology will continue to be the standard in higher-end digital cameras.

Resolution is measured in pixels. It is the amount of detail that the camera can capture. Basically, the more pixels, the more detail and better quality. With low resolution, pictures become "grainy" and look out of focus when enlarged.

The following is a list of resolutions used by digital cameras:

- **256 x 256 pixels**—Inexpensive cameras use this resolution. It produces a low-quality picture. It is 65,000 total pixels.

- **640 x 480 pixels**—This resolution is a little better. If you plan to e-mail most of your pictures or post them on a website, this resolution is adequate. It is 307,000 total pixels.

- **1216 x 912 pixels**—This resolution is in the "good" range. It is enough to print images in addition to e-mailing and posting. It is a "megapixel" image size—1,109,000 total pixels.

- **1600 x 1200 pixels**—This "high resolution" achieves good results when you print to larger sizes such as 8 x 10. It is almost 2 million total pixels.

Today, cameras with up to 10.2 million pixels are available, providing the same or even better results than film cameras.

Many digital cameras use an LCD screen that allows you to view and delete the pictures right away, as shown in Figure 6-6. The next step is transferring them to the computer.

Figure 6-6 LCD Screen on a Digital Camera

Cameras with fixed storage must be connected to the computer to download the images. This connection can be by serial, parallel, SCSI, or Universal Serial Bus (USB) port. Many newer cameras provide removable storage. It allows you to transfer the images to the computer or even directly to a printer with having to connect the camera.

The following list describes storage systems:

- **Built-in memory**—Used by many inexpensive cameras.
- **SmartMedia cards**—Small Flash memory modules.
- **CompactFlash**—Another form of Flash memory, similar to but slightly larger than SmartMedia cards.
- **Memory stick**—A proprietary form of Flash memory used by Sony.
- **Floppy disk**—Used by some cameras to store images.
- **Hard disk**—Small built-in hard disks, or PCMCIA hard-disk cards, for image storage.
- **Writeable CD and DVD**— Used by higher-end cameras.

You need a drive or reader to transfer files from Flash memory to your computer. These devices behave much like floppy drives and are inexpensive to buy. They let you transfer images to the computer without having to use cables.

The difference between storage media is their capacity: A floppy disk is fixed, whereas the capacity of Flash memory devices is increasing all the time.

Digital cameras use two main file formats: TIFF and JPEG. JPEG is a compressed format, and TIFF is an uncompressed format. The JPEG file format is more common for storing pictures, providing different quality settings such as medium or high.

Video cameras or camcorders have been around for almost 20 years. They are similar to a digital camera in that they use CCD. The lens in a camcorder shines the light onto CCD, which measures light with a half-inch (about 1 cm) panel of 300,000 to 500,000 tiny light-sensitive diodes called *photosites*.

The two types of video cameras are analog and digital. Analog camcorders record video and audio signals as an analog track on video tape. Every time you make a copy of a tape, it loses some image and audio quality. Analog formats lack a number of the impressive features you'll find in digital camcorders. The main difference between the available analog formats is what kind of video tape the camcorder uses and the resolution.

Analog formats include the following:

- **Standard VHS**—This format uses the same type of video tapes as a regular VCR. Once you record them, you can play them on a standard VCR.
- **VHS-C**—This format is a compact VHS format. The video camera tapes are smaller but can be played on a standard VCR with the use of an adapter.
- **Super VHS**—Super VHS tape records an image with 380 to 400 horizontal lines, a much higher-resolution image than that of standard VHS tape. The video camera itself is a VCR and can be connected directly to a television or VCR to copy to standard VHS tapes.

- **Super VHS-C**—This format is a more compact version of Super VHS that uses a smaller size cassette.

- **8 mm**—Small 8 mm tapes (about the size of an audio cassette) provide about the same resolution as standard VHS. The advantage is that this format allows for more compact video recorders, sometimes small enough to fit in a pocket. To view recordings, you attack the video recorder to the television.

- **Hi-8**—Similar to 8 mm camcorders, Hi-8 camcorders have a higher resolution—about 400 lines—and Hi-8 tapes are more expensive than ordinary 8 mm tapes.

Digital recorders, shown in Figure 6-7, record information digitally, as bytes. This process lets you reproduce the image to without losing any image or audio quality. You can also download digital video to a computer, where you can edit it or post it on the Internet. Also, digital video has a much better resolution than analog video, typically 500 lines.

Figure 6-7 Digital Video Recorder

The following are digital formats:

- **MiniDV**—These video recorders can be small and lightweight. They record on compact cassettes, which are fairly expensive and hold about 60 to 90 minutes of footage. The recordings have 500 lines of resolution and can be transferred to a personal computer. They have the ability to capture still pictures, just as a digital camera does. Sony has recently introduced MicroMV, a format that works the same basic way as MiniDV but records on much smaller tapes.

- **Digital8**—This format is produced by Sony exclusively. Digital8 recorders are similar to regular DV camcorders, but they use standard Hi-8mm tapes, which are less expensive and can hold up to 60 minutes of footage. You can copy Digital8 recordings without any loss in quality, and you can connect the recorders to a computer to download images for editing or Internet use.

- **DVD**—DVD video recorders are not as common compared to MiniDV models, but they will gain more acceptance. DVD recorders burn video information directly onto small discs. The advantage is that each recording session is recorded as an individual track, similar to the song tracks on a CD. These tracks allow you to jump to any section of video. DVDs can hold 30 minutes to two hours of video.

- **DVD-R and DVD-RAM**—The newer DVD video recorders support these two formats. DVD-R camcorder discs will work in most set-top DVD players. The disc can only be recorded to once. DVD-RAM allows you to record discs again and again, but they cannot be played in an ordinary DVD player. You connect the video recorder to the television to play recordings or you can copy them to another format.

- **Memory card**—Just like digital cameras, some digital video recorders can record directly onto solid-state memory cards, such as Flash memory cards, memory sticks, and SD cards.

Chapter 10

Printers and Printing

Printers are an important part of modern PC systems. Hard copies of computer and online documents are as important today as they were when the paperless revolution began several years ago. Modern computer technicians must be able to understand the operation of various types of printers so they can install and maintain them and troubleshoot printer problems.

The most common printers are electrophotographic-type laser printers and sprayed inkjet printers, as shown in Figure 10-1. Many offices and homes still use older impact-type dot matrix printers, but it is getting difficult to find replacement parts as these units break down.

Figure 10-1 Laser and Inkjet Printers

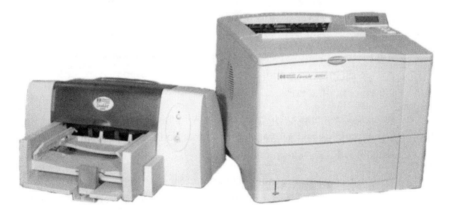

Some industries use thermal printers. They are a nonimpact type of printer that uses heat to transfer images to paper. The printhead contains small resistive heating pins that melt a wax-based ink onto plain paper or burn dots onto paper coated especially for the process.

There are two types of thermal transfer printers: direct thermal and thermal wax transfer. Direct thermal printers do not use ribbons. The printer prints the image by burning dots onto a specially coated paper as it passes over the heated printhead. Older fax machines used direct thermal printing.

Thermal wax transfer printers use a thermal transfer ribbon that contains a wax-based ink. The thermal printhead applies heat to the ribbon, which melts the ink. This process transfers ink to the paper, where it is permanent once it cools. A thermal transfer ribbon generally has three layers:

- The base material
- The heat-melting ink
- The coating on the print side of the base material

The coating and base material help keep ink from adhering to the printhead, which can cause poor print quality. Monochrome and color thermal transfer ribbons are available.

Another type of printer is dye-sublimation. Instead of using ink, dye-sublimation printers use a transparent film roll with solid dyes embedded. These solid dyes correspond to the four basic colors used in printing:

- Cyan
- Magenta
- Yellow
- Black

As the printhead heats up, it passes over the film, causing the dyes to vaporize and permeate the paper. The dyes then turn back to a solid, which leaves the color infused in the paper. Because the printers use a special glossy paper, the prints look like those from a photo lab. Additionally, various heat presses use dye-sublimation. For example, a reversed image is printed on the dye-sublimation printer and then used to transfer to a mug or T-shirt using a mug press or flat press.

Printers are connected to personal computers with Universal Serial Bus (USB), FireWire, serial, parallel, and network cable connections. Wireless types of connections include infrared and radio wave technology.

Printer drivers are software that you must install so the computer can communicate with the printer and coordinate the printing process. Printer drivers vary according to printer type, manufacturer, model, and PC operating system.

Print Quality and Resolution

Both inkjet and color laser printers can produce professional-quality photos, as shown in Figure 10-2. However, it is important to know that not all inkjet printers are equal. They are not all capable of professional-quality printing. Generally, the higher end the inkjet, the better the quality. Some inkjet printers are specially designed to produce top-quality photos, but these units tend to do poorly when printing text. The print quality is a factor of the resolution capabilities of the printer.

Figure 10-2 Inkjet Printers Produce Quality Photos

Print resolution refers to the number of tiny dots the print head is capable of fitting per inch when forming an image. For most laser printers in the market today, the standard resolution is 600 dots per inch (dpi). This resolution is sufficient for normal everyday printing, including small desktop publishing jobs. However, the high-end production printer might have a resolution of 2400 dpi. It is possible to find some laser printers that still use a resolution of 300 dpi. Note that this resolution can cause jagged lines on the outer edge of an image. Some manufacturers have created a solution for this. For example, the Hewlett-Packard Resolution Enhancement Technology (RET) is designed to correct this problem. RET works by inserting smaller dots at the edges of lines and smoothes the rough edges. Although RET does not improve the resolution, the printed document looks better.

The printer resolution is an important factor to consider when buying a printer or recommending the purchase of one by a customer. Always check the resolution to see how many dpi the printer is capable of. The higher the resolution, the better the image quality. Unless you require photo quality, the standard resolution of 600 x 600 is more than adequate for most printing. Also, check whether the printer offers a range of resolutions so the user can choose different resolutions for different printing jobs, such as draft mode.

Laser Versus Inkjet Printers

A laser printer is different from an inkjet in several ways. Figures 10-3 and 10-4 show a typical laser printer and inkjet printer. Apart from the cost difference, the following list details additional considerations:

- The toner or ink in a laser printer is dry. In an inkjet, it is wet.
- An inkjet printer is about 10 times more expensive to operate over time than a laser printer because ink needs replenishing more frequently.

- The printed paper from an inkjet printer might smear if it is wet. A laser printed document will not.

- An inkjet printer is sufficient if the printing needs are minimal. However, if printing volume is high, a laser printer is a better choice.

Figure 10-3 Laser Printer

Figure 10-4 Inkjet Printer

In terms of similarities, both inkjet and laser printers operate quietly and let you add fonts by using font cartridges or installing soft fonts.

Printer Accessories

You can use additional printer components to help the printing process for larger jobs. Most printers have a paper tray that holds a supply of paper as well as a sheet feeder for specialty printing. You can add extra paper trays to accommodate different sizes of paper, such as legal, executive, and envelopes, or different types, such as company letterhead. High-end printers often include a finisher that can collate and staple the paper. Options can include how the paper is sorted and where the staple is placed.

Combination printers that also fax, scan, and copy allow users to manage these functions using software that typically comes with the printer. The obvious advantage is that they use only one connection to the computer instead of taking up multiple ports.

Chapter 11

Preventive Maintenance

Firewalls

Many people are beginning to take advantage of the always-on feature of broadband technologies. Broadband users must be aware of the security risks associated with connecting a computer to the outside world. Security breaches on a home computer might allow a hacker to steal stored data or use the computer to hack into other computers.

You can take many steps to minimize the security risk of connecting a computer to the Internet. You can use a home firewall to prevent hacker attacks on a home computer. Firewalls are the most popular method of protecting corporate LANs from outside intruders. A firewall is a hardware or software system that is used to prevent unauthorized people from accessing sensitive data. A home firewall is normally located at the interface between the local devices and the high-speed broadband connection. The firewall examines all data, video, and voice traffic between these two networks. A typical home firewall system also does the following:

- Closes the broadband connection after detecting any attempts to hack into a digital appliance
- Allows different family members to set their own levels of security
- Records all broadband Internet access events

After installing a firewall, you need to open certain ports to use e-mail and the Internet. Simple Mail Transfer Protocol (SMTP) uses Port 25 and POP3 uses Port 110 to transmit and receive e-mail. You also need to open Port 80 for HTTP, the standard protocol that supports the exchange of information on the World Wide Web.

Windows XP has a built-in firewall called Internet Connection Firewall (ICF), which is shown in Figure 11-1. ICF is a software component that blocks unsolicited traffic from the Internet. ICF monitors all the outbound and inbound communications of a computer. If ICF does not recognize a packet being sent or received, the packet is dropped. Windows XP can create a plain-text log of all events, such as packets being dropped. ICF blocks all unsolicited incoming packets by default. If a computer is using an FTP server, click the **Services** tab in the **Advanced Settings** dialog box, as shown in Figure 11-2. Check the **FTP Server** box to allow this service through the ICF.

Figure 11-1 ICF Screen

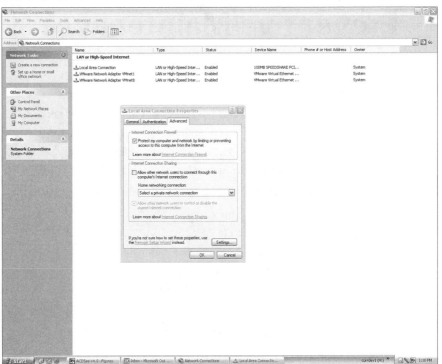

Figure 11-2 Advanced Settings

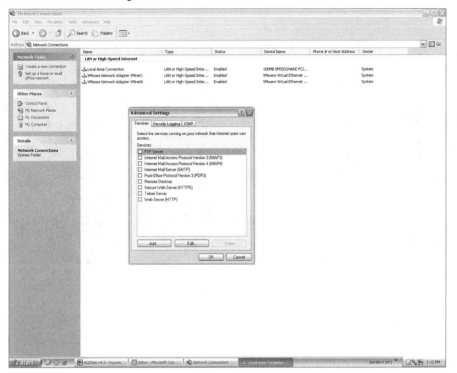

Chapter 13

Troubleshooting Software

Troubleshooting Windows XP Installation Problems

Some of the peripherals might not work correctly during the setup process. Begin troubleshooting by checking the system BIOS. An outdated BIOS can cause problems with disk partitioning, power management, peripheral configuration, and other important low-level functions. Identify the BIOS manufacturer and check whether an update is available. When the computer is using the most current version of the BIOS, go to the BIOS setup and select the option for a non–Plug-and-Play operating system. Even though Windows XP is a Plug-and-Play operating system, the BIOS option can prevent the Windows XP boot loader from accessing devices at startup. The BIOS option was intended for previous versions of Windows.

To boot the bootable CD during the installation process, go into the BIOS setup and change the boot sequence. You can configure the setting multiple ways, and each BIOS is different.

The system might crash after the text-mode setup is complete. This crash indicates that the setup is not compatible or that the driver for the disk subsystem is missing. If the computer comes with a high-performance Integrated Drive Electronics (IDE) controller or small computer system interface (SCSI) device, Windows XP might not include a compatible driver. The solution is downloading a driver that is compatible with Windows XP, coping the driver to a floppy disk, and rebooting the system. When the text-mode setup starts, look for the prompt at the bottom of screen to press F6 if third-party drivers must be installed. After the files are finished loading, setup prompts for the floppy disk containing the driver. After the driver is installed, Windows XP setup continues with the installation.

Windows XP Upgrade Issues

The issues that you encounter when upgrading to Windows XP are similar to the issues for performing Windows 9x, NT, and 2000 upgrades. As with Windows 9x, NT, and 2000, problems that occur during upgrades to Windows XP are either hardware or software related, and sometimes both hardware and software present problems. Before you begin any upgrade, consult the Microsoft website to see whether the hardware is compatible. Check with the manufacturer of the hardware components and software to see whether they have any updated drivers that are necessary for the upgrade. Microsoft recommends that you meet several requirements prior to installing the XP Home Edition operating system:

- A Pentium 233 MHz processor or faster, with 300 MHz recommended
- At least 64 MB of RAM, with 128 MB recommended
- At least 1.5 GB of available hard disk space
- A CD-ROM or DVD-ROM drive
- A keyboard and a Microsoft mouse or some other compatible pointing device
- A video adapter and monitor with Super VGA resolution of 800 x 600 or higher
- A sound card
- Speakers or headphones

Microsoft recommends that you meet several requirements prior to installing the Windows XP Professional operating system:

- A Pentium 233 MHz processor or faster, with 300 MHz recommended
- At least 64 MB of RAM, with 128 MB recommended
- At least 1.5 GB of available hard disk space
- A CD-ROM or DVD-ROM drive
- A keyboard and a Microsoft Mouse or some other compatible pointing device
- A video adapter and monitor with Super VGA resolution of 800 x 600 or higher
- A sound card
- Speakers or headphones

TIP

Make sure you know the minimum requirements for Windows XP Home and Professional.

Verify that your hardware meets the minimum recommendations for the upgrade. Microsoft has a list of recommendations on its website for the types of processors and amount of RAM that you need to run the selected operating system. It also includes recommendations for other hardware components.

Windows XP Startup Modes

The Windows XP operating systems provide a choice of startup modes just as the Windows 9x operating systems do. However, Windows XP has an advanced options menu that provides features in addition to the Safe Mode options.

Normal and Safe Mode Boot Modes

Windows XP allows users to boot normally or boot to Safe Mode, Safe Mode with Networking, or Safe Mode with Command Prompt. As with Windows 9x, Windows NT/2000 provides a means of booting the system into Safe Mode with minimal drivers to allow troubleshooting.

Enable Boot Logging

If you choose the Enable Boot Logging Startup mode, Windows creates a ntbtlog.txt file. It works in a similar fashion to the bootlog.txt file because it contains a list of all the drivers and services that the system attempts to load during the bootup process. Use this Startup Mode to determine what device or service is causing the system to fail.

Enable VGA Mode

Use the Enable VGA Startup mode if you experience any display problems while booting up. This mode loads the standard VGA driver instead of the driver for the video card. Boot into VGA mode and reconfigure the display setting with the Enable VGA mode Startup mode.

Last Known Good Configuration

If you load a new device driver and afterward the system begins to fail, use the Last Known Good Configuration Startup mode. It enables the system to start from the point of the last successful user logon without the new device drivers.

Windows XP Recovery Console

The Windows XP Recovery Console is a command-line interface you use to perform a variety of troubleshooting and recovery tasks. They include starting and stopping services, reading and writing data on a local drive (including drives that are formatted with the NT file system [NTFS]), and formatting hard disks. Once you start the Recovery Console, use the commands from the command line to remove, replace, or copy corrupt files.

TIP

Know how to use the Windows XP Recovery Console.

There is more than one way to start the Recovery Console. One way is to insert the Windows XP CD-ROM into the CD-ROM drive and wait for the Microsoft Windows XP CD dialog box to open. You will see the option to open the Recovery Console. Enter R to access it.

Another way is to go to the Run command window on the Start menu and type **cmd**. You will see the command-prompt window. Change to the drive letter of the CD-ROM and the **I386** folder, and run the **winnt32** command with the **/cmdcons** switch.

After you install the Recovery Console, you can access it from the menu called Please Select Operating System to Start.

fixmbr and fixboot

You can use the **fixmbr** command with the Recovery Console to fix hard-drive problems. The **fixmbr** command repairs a Master Boot Record (MBR). The syntax for this command is **fixmbr** *device_name*. If you omit the *device_name* parameter, fixmbr rewrites the MBR on the boot device. You can specify a device name to write a MBR to a different drive (such as a floppy disk or secondary hard disk). Use the **map** command to retrieve a list of device names. An example of a valid device name is MAP\Device\HardDisk0.

The **fixboot** command writes a new boot sector onto the system partition. The syntax for the command is **fixboot** *drive*:. If you do not specify the *drive*: option, fixboot writes the boot sector to the default boot partition. Specify a different drive if a boot sector is to be written to a volume other than the default boot partition.

Objectives

Upon completion of this chapter, you will be able to perform the following tasks:

- Windows XP and Windows NT/2000/Me/9x contrasts
- Windows XP versions
- Installing the Windows XP operating system
- Special installations

Appendix A

Windows XP Operating System

Windows XP is designed as an operating system for both the home and office. Microsoft released four different types of the XP operating system, including a Home Edition, a Media Center Edition, a 32-bit Professional Edition that is suitable for a large corporation or business environment, and a 64-bit Edition created for businesses with specialized and technical applications. (This book does not cover the version for the tablet PC.) This chapter briefly describes the different versions and lists some features new to Windows XP. Windows XP is built on the Windows 2000 code base and provides the same reliability and performance. Windows XP also enhances the new features of the Windows Me operating system, including System Restore, Windows Media Player, and Windows Image Acquisition. Microsoft designed Windows XP to replace Windows 98, Windows Me, and Windows 2000.

Windows XP Versions

Windows XP Home Edition

Windows XP Home Edition is a less-expensive version and is typically marketed to customers who use PCs in their homes and very small businesses. Figure A-1 shows a package of Windows XP Home Edition. Windows XP Home Edition serves inexperienced users who do not need to connect to corporate networks and do not require the extra security options that Windows XP Professional contains. Windows XP Home Edition is compatible with any desktop or notebook PC that has a single CPU and a video display.

Windows XP Home Edition includes many enhancements and features that are not included in Windows 2000 Professional or any of the previous Windows 9x releases. Some of these features include improved software and hardware compatibility, simplified security such as Simple File Sharing versus Windows 2000 Sharing, new logon screen, fast user switching, enhanced multimedia support, and DirectX multimedia libraries for gaming.

Figure A-1 Windows XP Home Edition

Windows XP Professional

The XP Professional operating system includes everything that the Home Edition provides, plus all the networking and security components that are required to join a Windows NT, 2000, or XP domain in a corporate network. XP Professional also includes support for high-performance hardware, such as a dual-processor motherboard. Figure A-2 shows a package of Windows XP Professional.

Figure A-2 Windows XP Professional

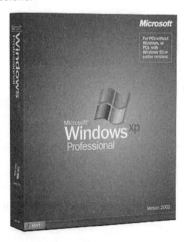

The kernel of Windows XP Home Edition and Windows XP Professional operating systems is identical. The file and folder management, web browser, and most of the system-management tools and troubleshooting tools are also the same. The digital media-management applications are not different from one another.

Windows XP Professional contains several features that are not included in Windows XP Home Edition:

- **Power user**—The new Remote Desktop feature allows mobile users to remotely access their corporate desktops. System administrators now have the capability to remotely administer clients on a network. *Automated System Recovery (ASR)* aids in system recovery from a catastrophic error that might render the system unbootable. Windows XP Professional, like Windows 2000 Professional, supports dynamic disks. The Home Edition supports only the standard Simple Disk type. Home Edition does not include the Internet Information Services (IIS) web server 5.1 software in the Windows XP Professional Edition.

- **Management**—Windows XP Professional provides added operating-system–management features. You can use the Professional Edition to log on to an Active Directory domain. The Professional Edition also supports group policies for domain users. Professional Edition includes a change and configuration management tool known as *IntelliMirror*. This tool includes user-managing data and the ability to centrally manage software installation, repair, updating, and removal.

- **Roaming profiles**—With Windows XP Professional, users can log on to any computer on the network and automatically receive their customized settings with Windows XP Professional. The user profile is stored in a shared network folder. When the user logs on to a machine, the information in the folder is copied over to the hard disk of the machine being used. When the user logs off, the profile information is copied back to shared network folder.

- **Corporate deployment**—Windows XP Professional is designed for use in corporate networks and contains support for multiple languages. XP Professional also provides *Sysprep support*, which you use to install the operating system on multiple machines in a large or corporate network.

- **Networking features**—Windows XP Professional provides networking features that you need when deploying the operating system in a large corporate network. These include Simple Network Management Protocol (SNMP), the user interface for IP Security (IPSec), SAP Agent, Client Service for NetWare, Network Monitor, and simple TCP/IP services.

Windows XP Professional contains additional security features. For example, each user in XP Home Edition is automatically assigned to the Owners local group. This group is the Windows XP equivalent of the Windows 2000 Administrator account. Anyone who logs on to a Home Edition machine has full control of the operating system. The Backup Operator, Power User, and Replicator groups do not exist in Windows XP Home Edition. However, the Windows XP Home Edition does include a Restricted Users group, which grants limited access to the operating system for selected users.

Windows XP Professional 64-Bit

Windows XP Professional 64-bit is Microsoft's first 64-bit operating system. This operating system is designed to accommodate specialized technical applications. For example, digital content creators including digital artists, 3D animators, gaming developers, and engineers can view more complex models and simulations to improve their products. Financial applications also benefit from the ability to calculate large sets of data in real time.

Windows XP 64-Bit Edition is also designed to address the most demanding business needs of today's Internet-based world, including e-commerce, data mining, online transaction processing, memory-intensive high-end graphics, complex mathematics, and high-performance multimedia applications. Note that 32-bit systems will continue to be the best environment for customers who use only 32-bit applications and do not work with data sets larger than 2 GB.

You must use a system built around an Intel Itanium 64-bit processor in conjunction with the 64-bit version of Windows XP Professional. This 64-Bit Edition also takes advantage of increased floating-point performance, which is the raw number of calculations that you can process in a given period of time using the Intel Itanium platform. XP Home Edition is unable to operate with this processor. Another advantage of the 64-Bit Edition is the memory support. The 64-Bit Edition currently supports up to 16 GB of RAM. One terabyte of system cache and a 512 terabyte page file are also supported as hardware and memory capabilities increase to 16 terabytes of virtual memory.

Windows XP 64-Bit Edition provides a scalable, high-performance platform for a new generation of applications that are based on the Win64 API. When compared to 32-bit systems, the Win64 API architecture provides more efficient processing of extremely large amounts of data and supports up to eight terabytes of virtual memory. With 64-bit Windows, applications can preload substantially more data into virtual memory to enable rapid access by the IA-64 processor. Table A-1 shows a comparison of 64-bit and 32-bit architectures.

Table A-1 Comparison of 64-Bit and 32-Bit Architecture

Address Space	64-Bit Windows	32-Bit Windows
Virtual memory	16 terabytes	4 GB
Paging file	512 terabytes	16 terabytes
System cache	1 terabyte	1 GB

You need a 64-bit motherboard and chip set for the Windows XP 64-bit Edition. Table A-2 shows a few minimum requirements.

Table A-2 Minimum Requirements for the Windows XP 64-Bit Edition

System Device	Minimum	Recommended
Processor 64-bit	733 MHz Intel Itanium	800 MHz Intel Itanium
Memory	1 GB RAM	1 GB RAM
Video	VGA	3-D graphics

Windows XP Media Center Edition

XP Media Center Edition is a new Microsoft edition that is preinstalled only on Media Center PCs, as shown in Figure A-3. It is designed to fulfill the needs of those users who want a powerful digital media center in their homes. The media center provides users with the ability to watch live television, record TV programs, listen to digital music, view slideshows and picture albums, and play DVDs all from one location, as shown in Figure A-4.

Figure A-3 Windows XP Media Center PC

Figure A-4 Windows XP Media Center PC

XP Media Center is a packaged hardware and software system built on the XP Professional platform to fulfill a user's personal computer needs. Some hardware that might comprise an XP Media Center computer includes an advanced graphics card; a TV tuner to capture a cable, antenna, or satellite signal and display it on the monitor; a hardware encoder to record the captured TV signal to the computer's hard disk; and a digital audio output that allows the digital audio of the PC to integrate into an existing home-entertainment system. This edition also includes a media-center remote control that is compatible with the computer through an infrared sensor located on the computer, along with the existing cable or satellite equipment.

Installing the Windows XP OS

Hardware Requirements

The hardware requirements for Windows XP depend upon the version of XP you install. Windows XP Professional requires more in terms of hardware capabilities than the Home Edition. Windows XP 64-bit encryption is optimized to enable customers to take advantage of the performance enhancements in the Intel Itanium 2 processor. Therefore, you need a more powerful computer, with hardware capable of handling the operating system without it operating too slowly or crashing.

This chapter refers to the system administrator more often than to the technician because Windows XP Professional, like Windows 2000, is more likely to run in a networked environment. Therefore, the system administrator will attend to most of the problems that occur.

Prior to installing Windows XP, ensure that the system hardware is capable of running the specific XP version you have. Microsoft recommends that you meet several requirements prior to installing the XP Home Edition operating system:

- A Pentium 233 MHz processor or faster, with 300 MHz recommended
- At least 64 MB of RAM, with 128 MB recommended
- At least 1.5 GB of available hard disk space
- A CD-ROM or DVD-ROM drive
- A keyboard and a Microsoft Mouse or some other compatible pointing device
- A video adapter and monitor with Super VGA resolution of 800 x 600 or higher
- A sound card
- Speakers or headphones

Microsoft recommends that you meet several requirements prior to installing the Windows XP Professional operating system:

- A Pentium 233 MHz processor or faster, with 300 MHz recommended
- At least 64 MB of RAM, with 128 MB recommended
- At least 1.5 GB of available hard disk space
- A CD-ROM or DVD-ROM drive
- A keyboard and a Microsoft Mouse or some other compatible pointing device
- A video adapter and monitor with Super VGA resolution of 800 x 600 or higher
- A sound card
- Speakers or headphones

Use the *Hardware Compatibility List (HCL)* before installing Windows XP to verify that the hardware will actually work with the OS. Microsoft provides drivers for only those devices included on this list. Using hardware that is not listed on the HCL might cause problems during and after installation. You can view the HCL by opening the hcl.txt file in the Support folder on the Windows XP Professional CD-ROM, as shown in Figure A-5.

Figure A-5 Windows XP HCL

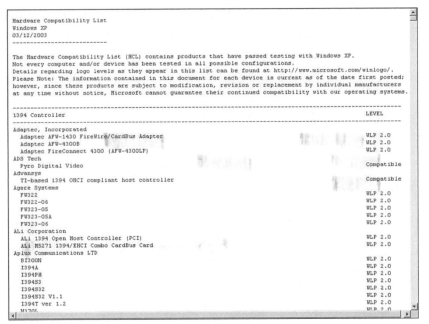

Windows XP Installation Steps

Before setting up Windows XP, you must first choose between the three types of installations:

- **Clean install**—Sets up a fresh copy of Windows XP. This new copy completely replaces any previous versions of Windows installed on the computer.

- **Upgrading an existing version**—Converts Windows 98, Windows 98 Second Edition, or Windows Me into Windows XP Home or Professional Edition. Windows Professional can be upgraded from Windows NT Workstation 4.0 with Service Pack 6 or Windows 2000 Professional with or without the service packs. Windows XP will not upgrade from Windows 3.1 or 95. You must perform a clean install.

- **Dual-boot installation**—Applies when you want to preserve the currently installed version of Windows. You must install the new version of Windows on a new partition separate from the current version. When the installation is complete, you can choose which operating system to boot from.

There are four main steps in the Windows XP installation process:

- File copy
- Text mode setup
- GUI mode setup
- Windows welcome

File Copy

This step copies the Windows setup files to a folder on the partition where they can run when the system is restarted. If you boot the system from a CD, setup skips this step and copies files directly from the CD.

Text Mode Setup

During a clean installation, you select the partition that the Windows XP system files will be installed into. You can create and format the partition in this step.

GUI Mode Setup

Windows setup uses a graphical wizard to guide you through the regional settings, product key, computer name, and administrator password.

Windows Welcome

As the last portion of the setup process, you have the option to create user accounts and activate Windows before using it for the first time.

 Lab 7.3.2 Installation Demonstration of Windows XP

In this lab, you learn how to install the Windows XP Professional operating system.

Files and Settings Transfer Wizard

With the help of the Files and Settings Transfer wizard, shown in Figure A-6, you can migrate settings and files from an old computer to a new computer. You can save settings from any 32-bit version of Windows, including Windows 95. Several options let you restore saved files and settings on Windows XP Home Edition or Professional Edition:

- You can make a direct connection with a serial cable between two computers.
- You can connect the computers over a network.
- You can compress and save files to removable media, such as a floppy disk, Zip disk, or CD-RW.
- You can use a removable drive or network drive to transfer data.

Figure A-6 Windows XP File and Setting Transfer Wizard

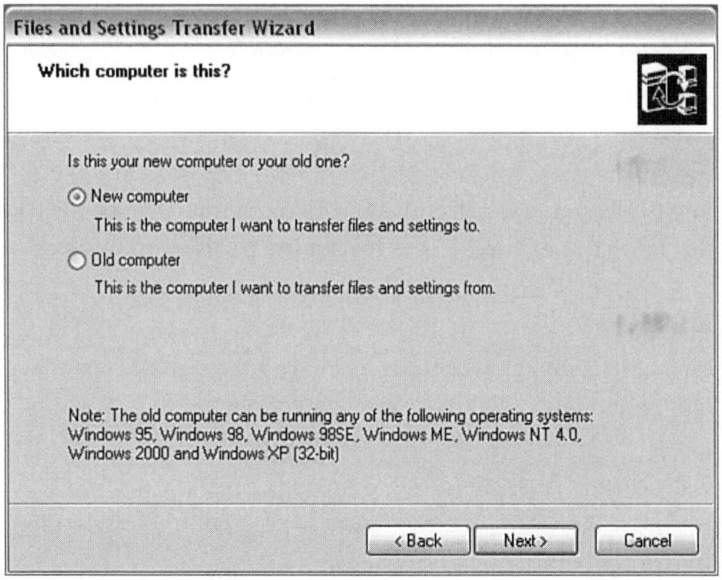

User State Migration Tool

The *User State Migration Tool (USMT)* is similar to the Files and Settings Transfer Wizard. The USMT is used by IT administrators who perform large deployments of Windows XP Professional in a corporate environment. USMT provides the same functionality as the wizard on a large scale for the purpose of migrating multiple users.

Activating Windows XP

Windows Product Activation (WPA) is a new feature included in Windows XP. As in previous versions of Microsoft Windows, you must enter a 25-character product key during the setup process. WPA requires you to activate the installation of Windows XP within 30 days after the installation. You can call a toll-free number and speak with a customer-service representative or connect to the Microsoft activation server over the Internet to complete this process. Users who purchase a packaged copy of Windows XP need to complete this process. The activation should take no longer than a few seconds over the Internet. However, the activation over the phone could take much longer because the representative provides you with a 42-digit confirmation ID that you must enter into the activation screen.

You can install Windows XP as many times as you need on the same hardware. When the product is activated, Windows XP transmits an encrypted file that serves as a unique identifier. This identifier includes a list of key components of the system, including the video card, primary hard disk, disk controller, CD-ROM drive, network adapter, CPU, and RAM. If you reinstall the copy of Windows XP on the same hardware, the activation server checks the identifier for a match to complete the activation.

If you change four or more components on the computer from a list of 10 within a 120-day period, the activation is rejected. you will be required to call the WPA and reactivate with a list of the new components. Windows activation is not a registration. This process is completely anonymous and does not send personal information to Microsoft. Optionally, you can choose to register the product.

Copies of Windows XP sold with new computers or sold to corporations might be exempt from the WPA requirements. The activation process might have already been completed for copies of Windows XP that are preinstalled on new computers. Businesses that purchase five or more copies of qualified Microsoft software including Windows XP receive volume-licensing media that do not require activation.

WPA was designed to protect against copying, which is the most common type of software piracy. The license entitles the user to install the software on a single computer. If someone uses the same CD and product key in a different computer, the activation will not occur. This feature makes the practice of sharing and distributing copies of software more difficult.

Special Installations

Upgrading to XP from Previous Windows Versions

Windows XP Home Edition or Professional Edition can upgrade from Windows 98, Windows 98 SE, or Windows Me. Windows NT Workstation 4.0 with Service Pack 6 and Windows 2000 Professional can also upgrade to Windows XP Professional. Windows 3.1 and Windows 95 cannot upgrade. You must first remove these operating systems and then perform a clean install.

To upgrade to Windows XP, boot up the current version of Windows and insert the Windows XP CD. Choose to install Windows XP. The Setup Wizard starts. This wizard is designed to make the installation an easy process. On the first page of the Setup Wizard, select **Upgrade** and click **Next**. Windows Setup Wizard then asks for a few items of information, including the product key, to complete the process. Setup then replaces the existing Windows files and saves the user settings, programs, and files that were previously installed on the computer. After several reboots, the installation is completed.

Upgrading from Windows NT Workstation 4 and Windows 2000

The process of upgrading a computer system from Windows NT 4.0 is actually quicker than performing a new install of Windows XP. Similar to the upgrade to Windows 2000, the computers that use Windows NT 4.0 or 2000 can connect and communicate with Windows XP computers. The Windows XP setup utility replaces the existing files with Windows XP files during the upgrade process. However, it saves the existing applications and settings. You should verify that the computers meet the hardware compatibility requirements to upgrade directly to Windows XP. You can use the HCL to determine whether a computer meets the necessary requirements.

Insert the Windows XP CD-ROM in the CD-ROM drive to start the upgrade procedure:

1. Choose **Start > Run**.

2. In the Run box, type **D:\i386\winnt32,** where D is the drive letter for the CD-ROM, and then press **Enter.**

3. The Welcome to the Windows XP Setup Wizard appears.

4. Select **Upgrade to Windows XP,** which is recommended, and click **Next.**

5. The License Agreement page appears.

6. Read the license agreement and click **I Accept This Agreement.**

7. Click **Next.**

8. The Upgrading to the Windows XP NTFS File System page appears.

9. Click **Yes, Upgrade My Drive,** and click **Next.**

10. The Copying Installation Files page appears.

11. The Restarting the Computer page appears and the computer restarts.

After the computer restarts, the upgrade process should continue without the need for any further user intervention.

Upgrading Windows 9x to Windows XP Professional

The process for upgrading Windows 9x to Windows XP is similar to the process of upgrading Windows 9x to 2000. Check the HCL to ensure that your computer will work with the Windows XP operating system.

If the computer passes the hardware-compatibility test, run the Windows XP setup program to start the upgrade to Windows XP:

1. Run the **xp.exe** command.

2. Accept the license agreement.

3. If the computer is already a member of a domain, create a computer account in that domain. Windows 95 and Windows 98 clients do not require a computer account. However, Windows XP Professional clients do.

4. Provide upgrade packs for any applications that might need them to work with Windows XP. Upgrade packs are available from the software manufacturer on the Internet. You have the option of visiting the Windows compatibility website to find the latest product updates and compatibility information during the upgrade process.

5. A prompt to upgrade to NT File System (NTFS) appears. Select this option unless the client computer will use dual-boot operating systems. This distinction is critical for dual-boot operating systems because FAT16 and FAT32 cannot recognize NTFS.

6. The Windows XP compatibility tool runs and generates a report. If the report shows the computer is Windows XP compatible, continue with the upgrade. If the report shows the computer is incompatible with Windows XP, terminate the upgrade process and either remove the incompatible device or upgrade the device.

7. The upgrade should finish without further user intervention. After the upgrade is finished, you must enter the password for the local computer administrator account.

If the computer is Windows XP compatible, it is now upgraded and it is a member of the domain. Figure A-7 demonstrates the process of upgrading Windows 9x to Windows XP.

Figure A-7 Upgrading to Windows XP

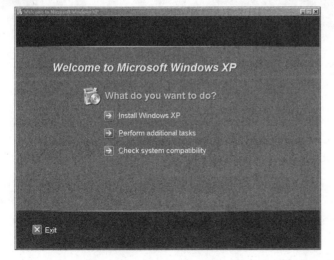

You must restart the system for the installation process to finish. After the system reboots, the installation proceeds through a typical Windows XP installation, as discussed earlier.

Dual-Boot Windows 9x, Windows NT 4, Windows 2000, and Windows XP

You can set up Windows XP to dual boot with another Windows operating system such as Windows 98 or Windows 2000. When the computer system is set up for a dual boot, a menu offers choices of different operating systems to use during startup. To dual boot the system, do a fresh install of Windows 98 before installing Windows XP. Figure A-8 shows a startup screen that has options for booting into two different operating systems.

Figure A-8 Dual Booting Windows XP

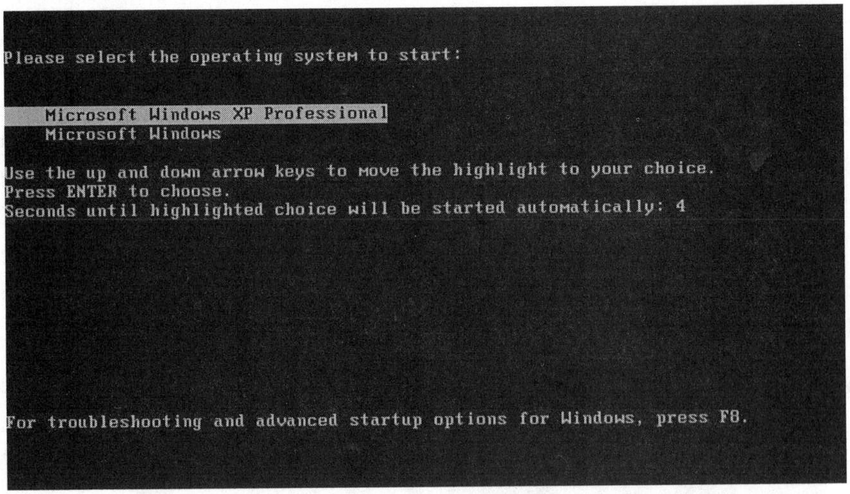

In this example, the Microsoft Windows 2000 Professional Setup option starts Windows 2000, and the Microsoft Windows option starts Windows XP.

Note that if the system is set up as dual boot, you cannot use any of the applications that are installed in the other operating system partition. If you need to use the same application in both operating systems, you must install it in each operating system.

If the operating systems have incompatible file systems, you can create two separate partitions. You can install an operating system on each partition. Alternatively, you can create separate logical drives and install the two operating systems onto them.

However, if the hard drive is formatted with NTFS, the Windows 98 operating system cannot read files in the Windows 2000 NTFS partition. Microsoft recommends that both partitions be formatted with the FAT file system if the computer is set up to dual boot with Windows 98 and 2000. Windows 2000 can operate with the FAT file system and read files in the other partition.

Windows XP and Windows NT/2000/Me/98/95 Contrasts

System Tools

Chapter 6, "Multimedia Capabilities," covered the Administrative Tools utility in detail. This utility is a powerful system tool, unique to Windows NT, 2000, and XP, that enables you to control just about everything related to the local computer. From this utility, you can control permission to log on to the computer through local user accounts.

Keeping User Files Private

When a user upgrades from Windows 98 or Windows Me, the setup program automatically creates a user account with no password. To add a password to the user account, open **Control Panel** and click **User Accounts.** A dialog box gives you the opportunity to make your files and folders private.

NOTE

If the user profile is stored on a FAT 32 drive, this option does not appear.

The NTFS provides the option of making files and folders private so that only the user has access to them. XP has the ability to make all or a selected few folders private. Suppose a user wants a roommate to have access to the My Documents folder but not certain files in the folder. The user can create a subfolder in My Documents and make it private. The user can put any files he does not want the roommate to access in the private subfolder. Previously in Windows 2000, you implemented this privacy with rights and permissions on files and folders.

Figure A-9 shows that the file system is formatted with NTFS. Right-click the local disk drive C:, select **Properties,** and look under **File System** to determine whether the partition has been formatted with NTFS.

Figure A-9 Hard Drive Formatted with NTFS

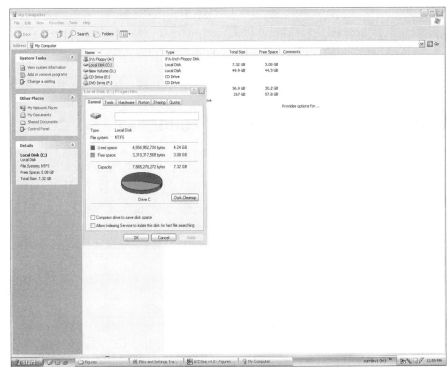

Simple File Sharing Versus Windows 2000 Sharing

File and resource security is another feature of Windows XP. Windows XP uses a system called *Simple File Sharing*. This system provides a stripped-down interface that eases the setup of common security arrangements. Simple File Sharing differs from classic Windows NT and 2000 file sharing in several ways, as shown in Figures A-10 and A-11.

Figure A-10 Simple File Sharing

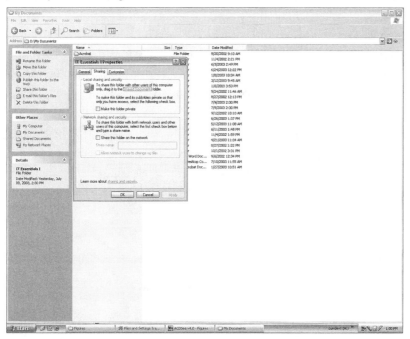

Figure A-11 Classic File Sharing

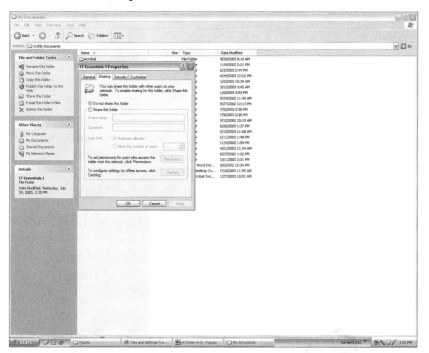

In Windows XP, you set permissions for local users and network users at the folder level only. Windows XP cannot apply permissions to individual files. Network users who connect to a computer are authenticated using that computer's guest account. The guest account provides only those privileges and permissions that apply to the computer that is being accessed or shared. Windows XP also provides an option to switch from the Windows XP interface to the classic Windows 9x or 2000 interface according to the user's preference.

In the XP Home Edition, Simple File Sharing is the only option. In XP Professional, both interfaces are available. The user can switch between these interfaces in **Control Panel** > **Appearance** > **Themes** > **View** by selecting or clearing the last item in the Advanced Setting box. Simple File Sharing is the default setting.

 Lab 7.5.2 Using Simple File Sharing to Share Files

In this lab, you use the Simple File Sharing techniques and tools that are new to Windows XP to share resources in a Windows XP network.

Internet Enhancements

The Internet Enhancements feature is new to the Windows XP environment. Windows XP shipped with Explorer 6, which is the most recent version of Microsoft's Internet browser, shown in Figure A-12. Explorer 6 integrates streaming media playback tools into the task pane on the left side of the browser. Windows XP provides a control to protect privacy. This control enables you to build a custom policy that can block or allow cookies on a site-by-site basis.

A cookie is a small text file stored on the PC's hard disk, which allows a website to track the user's personal association to that particular site. You can use some settings in Internet Explorer to manage cookies through **Tools** > **Internet Options** > **Privacy**. On the Privacy tab, select the desired cookie control of choice with the slider tab on the left. Some websites might not function properly if you select Block All Cookies. To view a nonfunctioning site, choose a lower cookie setting.

XP also comes with an Internet Connection Firewall (ICF) built in to stop the most common attacks. This feature is significant for users with high-speed Internet connections such as cable and DSL modems that are on 24 hours a day. Chapter 12 of *IT Essentials I: PC Hardware and Software Companion Guide* provides more information on firewalls.

Figure A-12 Internet Explorer 6

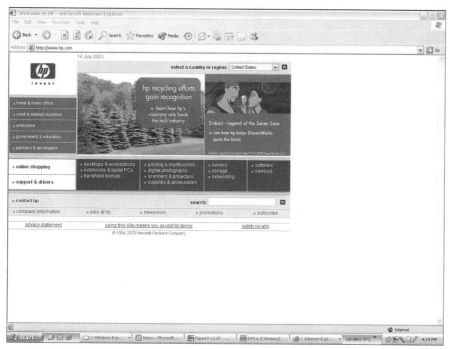

Remote Desktop Connection

Remote Desktop uses a Terminal Services technology that allows the user to work on a Windows XP Professional computer from any other computer. Suppose a user worked from home the night before and forgot to bring the file to work the next day. By logging on remotely to the home PC, the user can access the entire file and navigate the computer as if she were sitting in front of it.

To set up Remote Desktop, you must connect two computers through a LAN or a dial-up or high-speed Internet connection. The computer that you want to control is the *remote* computer, and the computer used to control it is the *client* computer. The remote computer must be operating under Windows XP Professional and have a known public IP address. The client computer must be operating under a version of Windows, such as XP, 2000, Me, 98, 95, or NT. For the remote connection to work on machines that do not have Windows XP, you must install client software from the Windows XP Professional CD. Also, the client machine must have access through a LAN, virtual private network (VPN), or dialup line to take advantage of the Remote Desktop option. Figure A-13 shows the Remote Desktop Connection interface.

Figure A-13 Remote Desktop Connection

 Lab 7.5.3a Remote Desktop Connection

In this lab, you use the Remote Desktop Connection of Windows XP to establish a remote connection to another computer.

 Lab 7.5.3b Internet Connection Firewall

In this lab, you use the ICF feature of Windows XP to ensure greater computer security.

System Properties

The System Properties dialog box is a new feature in Windows XP. This dialog box has new tabs, including Automatic Updates, Remote, and System Restore. These new features give the user added reliability and troubleshooting methods.

To access the System Properties dialog box, right-click My Computer and select Properties.

Automatic Update Tab

Automatic Update, as shown in Figure A-14, allows the user to configure when and how Windows Update checks for critical updates. In addition to the option to turn off Automatic Update completely, three types of notification settings appear:

- **Notify Me Before Downloading Any Updates and Notify Me Again Before Installing Them on My Computer**—This notification prompts the user by displaying an icon in the system tray. At that time, you have the option to download or reject the update. If accepted, the Automatic Update prompts you again to install or reject the update. This setting is for users with a dialup Internet connection who do not want to slow the Internet connection with an update download.

- **Download the Updates Automatically and Notify Me When They Are Ready to Be Installed**—This option notifies you when the update is downloaded and available to install. This setting is most useful for a high-speed always-on Internet connection.

- **Automatically Download the Updates and Install Them on the Schedule That I Specify**—This setting fully automates the updating process.

Figure A-14 Automatic Update

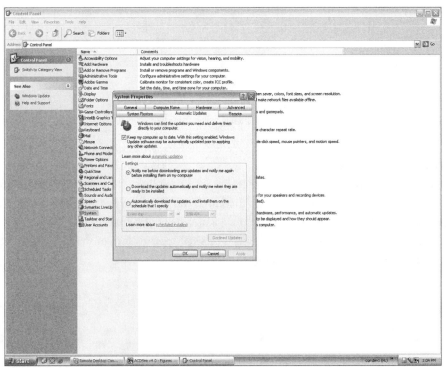

Remote Tab

The Remote tab, shown in Figure A-15, contains two new features: Remote Assistant and Remote Desktop. XP Home Edition includes the Remote Assistant feature. Both features are included with XP Professional.

Figure A-15 Remote Access Tab

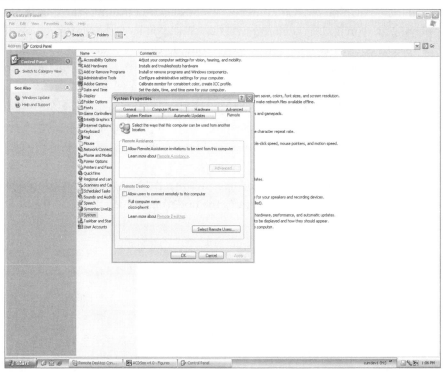

Remote Assistant

Remote Assistant is a convenient troubleshooting tool that allows administrators to connect to a client machine across any distance over the Internet. Remote Assistant can create a secure, reliable connection to ensure that neither computer is compromised. The interface hides the complexity of the process to let you navigate with ease. The Remote Assistant page appears in Figure A-16.

Figure A-16 Remote Assistance SC

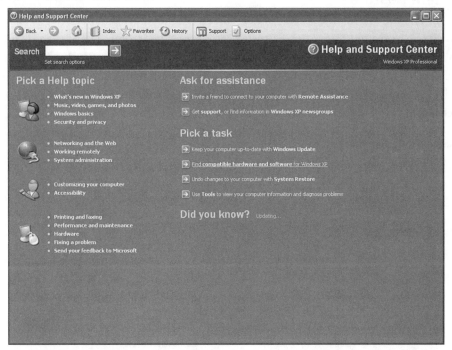

To enable Remote Assistant, two parties must establish a session. These parties are known as the *novice* and the *expert*. Both parties must be using Windows XP for this connection to work. Also, both parties must have active Internet connections or be on the same local network. The connection is not established if third-party firewalls are blocked. If the XP Internet Connection Firewall is the only firewall in use, Windows XP automatically opens the port when the user requests a Remote Assistance connection.

There are three steps to establishing a Remote Assistance connection:

1. The novice sends an invitation through Windows Messenger or e-mail.

2. The expert accepts the invitation, which opens a terminal window that displays the desktop of the novice machine.

3. The terminal window is read-only for the expert. If the novice chooses to enable the Allow Expert Interaction option, the expert can manipulate the novice machine.

The expert can communicate with the novice through text chat or voice chat.

System Restore

System Restore is a Windows XP service that runs in the background. This service allows you to restore the operating system at a predefined point. The System Restore tab is located in the System Properties dialog box, as shown in Figure A-17. This feature keeps a log of the continual changes in folders, files, and settings that are crucial to the operating system. These logs are stored in **%SystemRoot%\System32\Restore\ Filelist.xml.**

Figure A-17 System Restore Tab

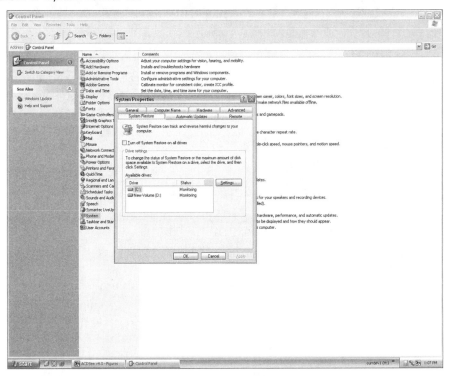

The system files are copied to hidden archives for security at regular intervals. System Restore also takes snapshots of the system state, including user accounts, hardware and software settings, and startup files, at regular intervals. Windows XP creates an initial restore point whenever an install or upgrade takes place. Also, it creates restore points every 24 hours, regardless of user activity, if you leave the computer on. If you turn off the computer and more than 24 hours passes since the prior restore point, the service creates a restore point when the computer is turned on. Windows XP also allows you to create a restore point manually at any time.

Restore points are automatically created during several actions:

- You install an unsigned device driver.
- You install an application that uses an installer which is compatible with System Restore.
- You install a Windows update or patch.
- You restore the system to a prior configuration using System Restore.
- You restore a backup set that was created with the Windows XP backup program.

System Restore does not monitor certain files or folders, including page files; any files stored in the personal data folders such as My Documents, Favorites, Recycle Bin, History, or Temporary Internet Files; images and graphics files; Microsoft Outlook and Outlook Express e-mail files; and files that use extensions commonly associated with data files, such as .doc, .xls, .mbd, or .pdf.

If a problem causes Windows XP to not function properly, you can start the System Restore Wizard in Safe Mode as well as in normal mode. You can then set the system back to a previous working date. This new service to XP can be extremely helpful when conflicts with drivers arise and when the system stops working for an undetermined reason.

A driver might not work for one of two reasons. First, a new program can conflict with the installed driver. Second, you might install a new driver that causes instability in the system. When the system suddenly stops working, you can select a restore date prior to the problem, and the system will return to normal operation.

System Restore cannot protect against viruses, worms, or a Trojan horse. Once they are detected, you might have a difficult time determining how long a virus has been in the system and what files it has infected. System Restore could actually restore the virus, even thought the objective is to remove it. Be sure to use and update your antivirus software.

Newly Designed Graphical Interface

Windows XP has a new graphical user interface (GUI), as shown in Figure A-18. The Start menu, the Task Manager, and the taskbar remain. However, the icons for My Computer, Network Places, and My Documents no longer appear on the desktop by default. The Start menu has a different appearance, when compared to earlier versions of Windows. The Start menu now includes access to My Computer, Network Places, and so on. This change allows you to more easily access these directories when other windows are open on the desktop. You can customize the Start menu to display shortcuts to the most commonly used items. The logon and logoff user icons were updated as well.

Figure A-18 Windows XP GUI

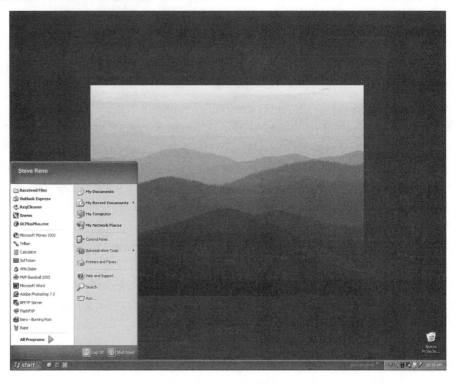

With previous versions of Windows, the taskbar became cluttered if you opened multiple windows. Windows XP organizes common items into groups on the taskbar, such as word-processing files, spreadsheet files, and so on. Clicking an item on the taskbar opens a pop-up menu that displays the files in use for the application.

Windows XP has new visual styles and themes that can be easily related to specific tasks:

- **Brighter colors**—Windows XP is capable of displaying color settings of 24-bit and 32-bit true color because of advances in video-card technology. Windows XP uses these enhanced color features to offer brighter and bolder color schemes than used in previous Windows versions.

- **3-D windows and buttons**—The Windows XP GUI appears to have a 3-D look; the windows and buttons have rounded edges and smooth shadows. Buttons, tabs, and windows shift colors as the mouse moves over them.

- **Sharper icons**—Microsoft has completely redesigned all the icons to make them brighter and stand out more. You can change the properties of these icons to make them appear about twice as large as in previous versions of Windows. Windows XP includes an option to view the large icons in a Titles View, which adds a few lines of detailed information about the icon.

- **Integrated themes**—You can save schemes, fonts, sizes, and sounds in Windows XP. Theme support is tightly woven into the Windows XP Control Panel Display utility. You can change window borders, common controls, and menus as well. Desktop themes were first introduced in the Plus Pack add-in to Windows 95.

Putting Pictures on Folder Icons

Folder icons in Windows XP provide a preview of the folder contents in the thumbnail view, as shown in Figure A-19. For example, a folder icon displays the art from a music CD that was extracted to the hard drive. A folder that contains pictures displays a preview of up to four of those pictures on the folder icon. When a folder contains videos, the folder icon displays the first frame of up to four videos. You can access the preview option from the Folder Properties dialog box on the Customize tab.

Figure A-19 Pictures on the Folder

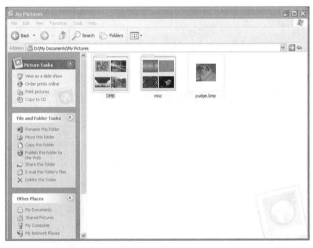

Fast User Switching

On a shared work or home computer, you have the capability to switch quickly between accounts without having to log off. This capability was initially designed for home use. It is enabled by default with the Windows XP Home Edition. Fast user switching is also available on Windows XP Professional if it is installed on a standalone or workgroup-connected computer. If you join a domain with a computer that uses Windows XP Professional, you cannot use fast user switching.

Suppose two users share one computer, and the first user is downloading music. The second user has the ability to check his e-mail without disrupting the music download of the first user. Both users have the ability to share with no logoff time delay.

Windows XP takes advantage of Terminal Services technology and operates each user session as a unique Terminal Services session. This technique keeps each user's data entirely separate.

Enhanced Networking Features

Windows XP incorporates features that are compatible with the latest advances in networking technology. For example, wireless access enhancements follow the IEEE 802.11b standard.

All New Windows Explorer

Windows XP improved Windows Explorer. Windows XP incorporated a new organized approach with its new appearance, as shown in Figure A-20. When a folder window is open, the Folder button toggles the left pane between the familiar folders tree and the new task pane. This pane consists of a set of links that offer quick access to common tasks, related locations, shortcuts, and details. You can easily see the new tiles view can be seen in the My Computer window.

Figure A-20 Windows Explorer

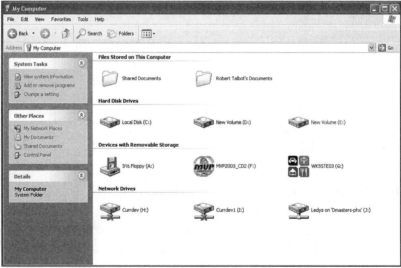

Windows Explorer takes a more organized approach to browsing folders and files. For example, the folders, hard drives, removable storage devices, and network places in My Computer are all grouped in categories.

You can better organize the files in My Documents by arranging them in various groups. You can also view your documents by type or group files according to the last modification date.

Windows XP uses Webview technology to better manage files and file namespace. For example, a selected file or folder has a list of options available, which allow you to rename, move, copy, e-mail, remove, or publish it to the web. This functionality is similar to Windows 2000. If you right-clicks on a file or folder, Windows XP displays this information directly on the desktop.

Windows XP introduces an easier-to-manage taskbar by grouping multiple instances of the same application. For example, instead of having nine instances of a Microsoft Word file each arranged horizontally on the taskbar, Windows XP groups them together on one taskbar button. In this scenario, you see only one taskbar button, showing the number of files that are open for the application. Clicking the button shows the vertical list of all filenames. In addition, the files can all be cascaded, tiled, or minimized at the same time.

New Logon

Windows XP provides a new logon procedure, as shown in Figure A-21. If you set up a profile on the system, you can click the icon by the correct name and type in the password. An administrator cannot log on from this screen. By default, you access the administrator account by pressing the **Ctrl-Alt-Del** buttons twice.

Figure A-21 Windows XP Logon Screen

Windows XP can display a photo or other image beside the names of account holders on the Welcome screen. Although an administrator of an account can assign pictures for all users, any account holder can choose his or her own picture.

 Lab 7.5.5 Using Windows XP's Start Menu and Windows Explorer

In this lab, you explore the basic features of the Windows XP Start menu and Windows Explorer navigation tools.

Summary

This chapter discussed the Windows XP operating systems. You must retain several important concepts from this chapter:

- Windows XP features Simple File Sharing, Internet enhancements, and a new GUI.
- The four different editions of Windows XP covered in this chapter include the Home, XP Professional, Professional 64-Bit, and Media Center Editions.
- Similar to working with Windows 2000, you must verify that the system is compatible with the Windows XP operating system. Use the HCL before installing Windows XP to verify that the hardware will work with the operating system.
- The three types of installations are a clean installation, an upgrade, and a dual-boot installation.
- The minimum hardware requirements for Windows XP Professional include a Pentium 233 MHz processor or faster, with 300 MHz recommended; at least 64 MB of RAM, with 128 MB recommended; at least 1.5 GB of available hard disk space; and a CD-ROM or DVD-ROM drive.
- The User State Migration Tool (USMT) is used by IT administrators who are performing large deployments of Windows XP Professional in a corporate environment. USMT provides the same functionality as the Files and Settings Transfer Wizard on a large scale for migrating multiple users.
- Windows XP includes a new feature called Windows Product Activation (WPA) that requires you to activate the installation within 30 days.
- The process of upgrading a computer system from Windows NT 4.0 to Windows XP is actually quicker than performing a new install of Windows XP. Similar to the upgrade to Windows 2000, the computers that use Windows NT 4.0 or 2000 can connect and communicate with Windows XP computers.

Key Terms

Automated System Recovery (ASR)   A tool that aids in system recovery from a catastrophic error that might render the system unbootable.

Hardware Compatibility List (HCL)   A text file that you can view before installing Windows XP to verify that the hardware will actually work with the operating system.

IntelliMirror   A change and configuration management tool that includes user-managing data functions and the tools to centrally manage software installation, repair, updating, and removal.

Remote Assistant   A convenient troubleshooting tool that allows you to connect to a client machine across any distance over the Internet.

Remote Desktop Connection   A Terminal Services technology that allows you to work on a Windows XP Professional computer from any other computer. By logging on remotely to the home PC, you can access the files and navigate the computer as if you were sitting in front of it.

Simple File Sharing   This system provides a stripped-down interface that eases the setup of common security arrangements. Simple File Sharing differs from classic Windows NT and 2000 file sharing.

System Restore   A Windows XP service that runs in the background and allows you to restore the operating system at a predefined point.

Sysprep support   A tool that you use to install the operating system on multiple machines in a large or corporate network.

User State Migration Tool (USMT)   Similar to the Files and Settings Transfer Wizard, the USMT is used by IT administrators who are performing large deployments of Windows XP Professional in a corporate environment. USMT provides the same functionality as the wizard on a large scale for the purpose of migrating multiple users.

Windows XP Operating System Labs

The following table maps the numbering scheme in this chapter's labs to the target indicators (TIs) in the online curriculum.

Lab Numbering	Online Curriculum TI
Lab B-1	7.3.2
Lab B-2	7.5.2
Lab B-3	7.5.3a
Lab B-4	7.5.3b
Lab B-5	7.5.5

Lab B-1: Installation Demonstration of Windows XP

Estimated Time: 90 Minutes

Objective

In this exercise, you learn how to install the Windows XP Professional Edition operating system.

Equipment

You need the following equipment for this lab:

- A computer with a blank hard disk
- A Windows XP Professional Edition installation CD

Scenario

The IT department has decided to upgrade all the end-user computers to Windows XP Professional. You need to reinstall the operating systems.

Procedures

In this lab, you learn how to install the Windows XP Professional Edition operating system.

Step 1

1. Insert the CD into the CD-ROM drive.

2. Configure the system BIOS boot sequence to boot from the CD-ROM first. Keep the CD in the drive and restart the computer.

3. When the system starts up, watch for the message **Press Any Key to Boot from CD**. When the message appears, press any key on the keyboard to boot the system from the CD. The system begins inspecting the hardware configuration, as shown in Figure B.1.

Figure B.1 Inspecting the Hardware Configuration Screen

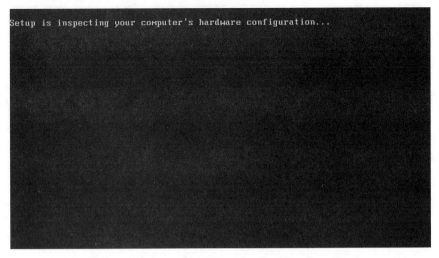

4. Next, the Windows XP setup screen displays and prepares the installation program to load the necessary files, as shown in Figures B.2, B.3, and B.4.

Figure B.2 Windows XP Setup Screen: Screen 1

Figure B.3 Windows XP Setup Screen: Screen 2

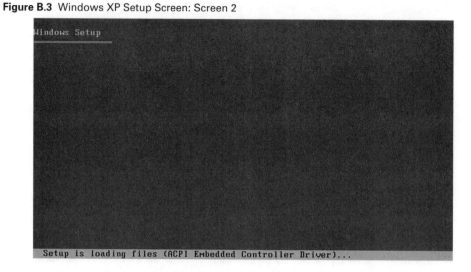

Figure B.4 Windows XP Setup Screen: Screen 3

5. These screens displays for a few minutes while the files are copied to the hard drive.

The Welcome to Setup screen displays next, as shown in Figure B.5. Press **Enter** to continue with the installation.

Figure B.5 Welcome to Setup Screen

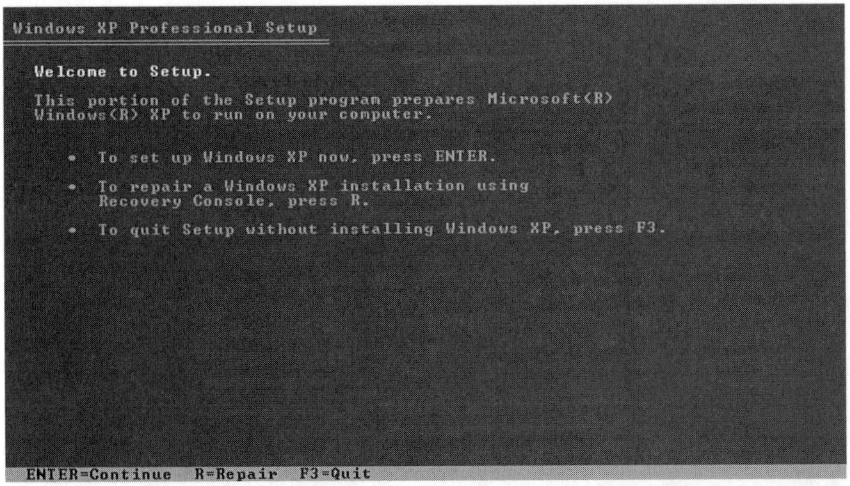

6. After the Windows XP Licensing Agreement screen displays (see Figure B.6), press **F8** to agree with the licensing agreement and continue with the installation.

Figure B.6 Windows XP Licensing Agreement Screen

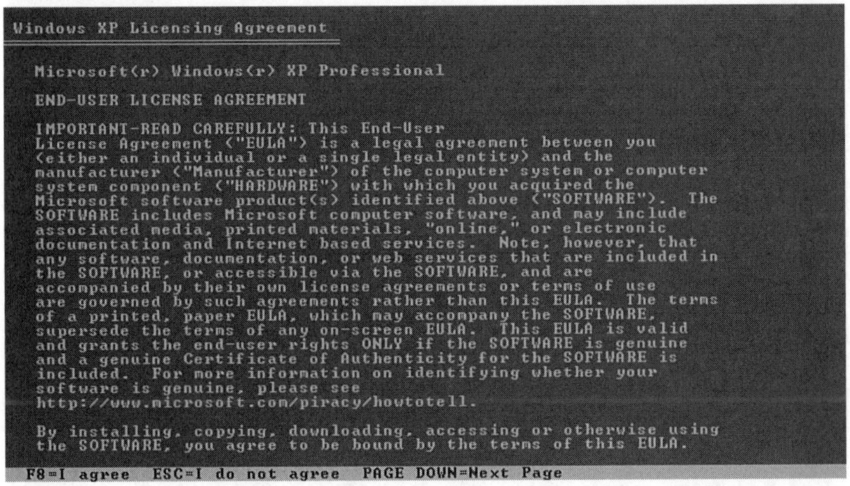

7. The next step is to partition and format the hard drive. This step is not always required. If you have a partition already created, use the arrow keys to scroll to that partition. Then, press **Enter** to install the operating system on that partition. If you do not need to create a partition, create a small partition to install Windows XP. Such a step makes the installation process faster.

To begin the partition setup process, press **C** to create a new partition in the unpartitioned space, as shown in Figure B.7.

Figure B.7 Partition Setup Screen: Screen 1

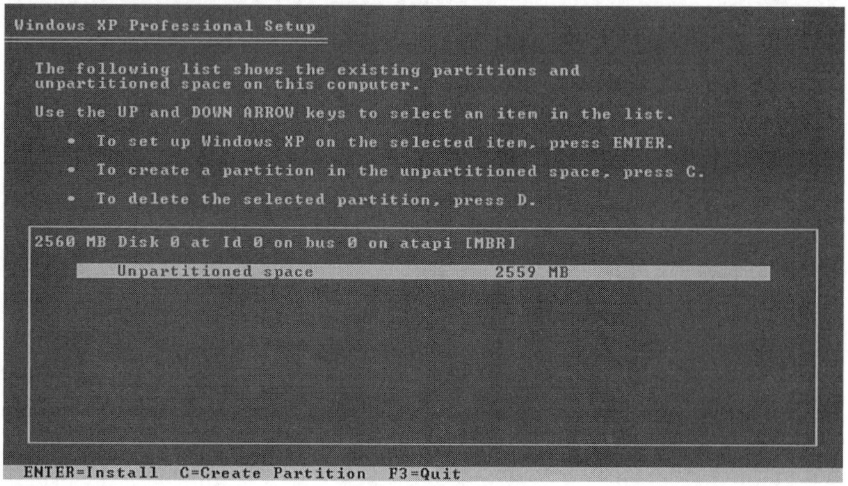

8. In the space provided, type **2555** to create a 2555 MB partition, as shown in Figure B.8. Then, press **Enter** to continue with the installation.

Figure B.8 Partition Setup Screen: Screen 2

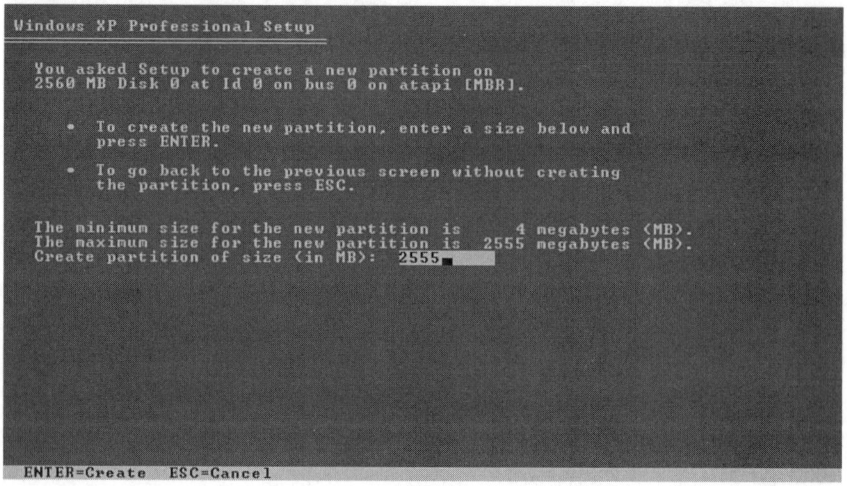

9. For the next step, press **Enter** to select the option to install the operating system on the partition that you just created. It should be the **C** drive, as shown in Figure B.9.

Figure B.9 Select Partition Screen

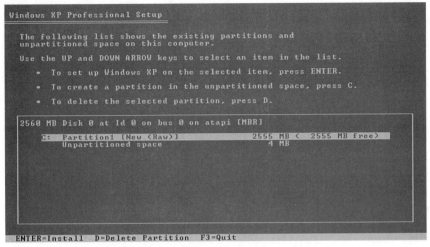

10. Select the option to format the partition using the NT file system (NTFS) (see Figure B.10). Do not use the quick method.

Figure B.10 Format Partition Screen

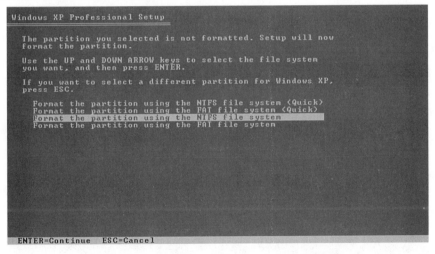

Setup begins formatting the partition, as shown in Figure B.11.

Figure B.11 Formatting Partition Screen

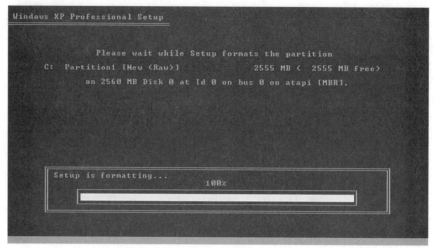

When the partitioning and formatting is complete, the Windows XP Professional Setup screen displays and starts copying the system files to the hard drive, as shown in Figures B.12 and B.13.

Figure B.12 Windows XP Professional Setup Screen: Screen 1

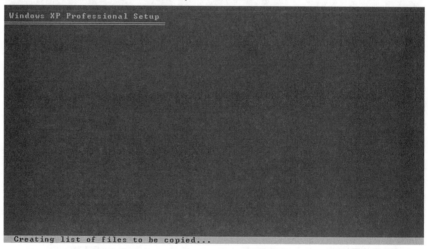

Figure B.13 Windows XP Professional Setup Screen: Screen 2

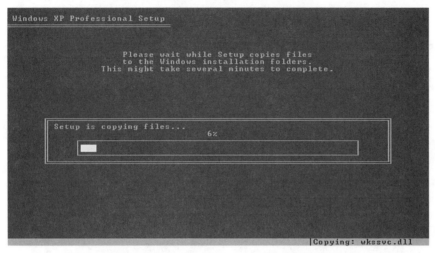

11. The system restarts automatically when the files have been copied. When the system restarts, the message **Press Any Key to Boot from CD** displays again. Do not press any keys at this time.

The Windows XP splash screen then displays, as shown in Figure B.14.

Figure B.14 Windows XP Professional Splash Screen

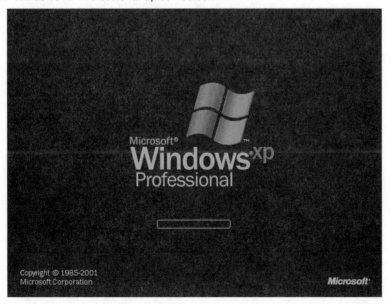

The Windows XP installation screen displays and begins installing the operating system, as shown in the Figure B.15.

Figure B.15 Windows XP Installation Screen

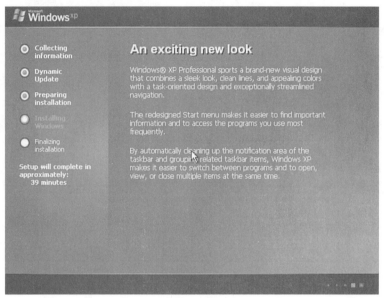

The next step of the installation begins installing the hardware devices. Setup proceeds to the screen shown in Figure B.16.

Figure B.16 Windows XP Installing Devices Screen

12. After the devices are initialized and installed, setup proceeds to the Regional and Language Options screen, as shown in Figure B.17. Here, you can customize the installation based on which country you live in or the language you speak.

Figure B.17 Regional and Language Option Screen

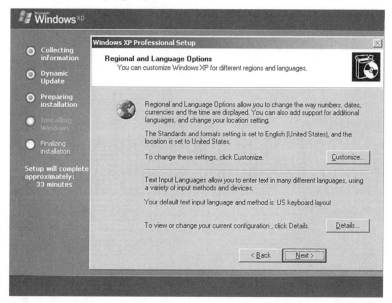

13. After making the proper selections, press **Enter** and proceed to the Personalization screen, as shown in Figure B.18.

Figure B.18 Personalization Screen

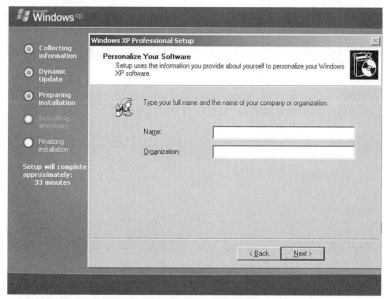

14. When this screen appears, type in the username on the first line and the organization on the second line. Check with the instructor when you reach this point. He or she might have a specific name and organization for you to type in.

15. Press the **Next** button when finished. The next page to appear is the Product Key page.

    Enter the Windows XP product key that came with the installation CD. Then, press the **Next** button to continue.

    The next screen to appear is the Computer Name and Administrator Password page, as shown in Figure B.19.

Figure B.19 Computer Name and Administrator Screen

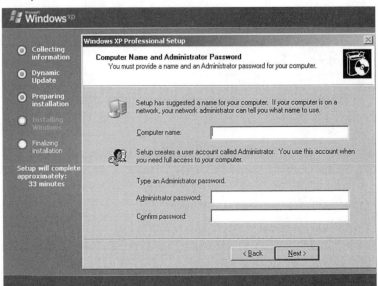

16. Enter the computer name on the top line and the administrator password on the bottom two lines. Click **Next**.

    The next page to appear is the Date and Time Settings page, as shown in Figure B.20.

Figure B.20 Date and Time Settings Screen

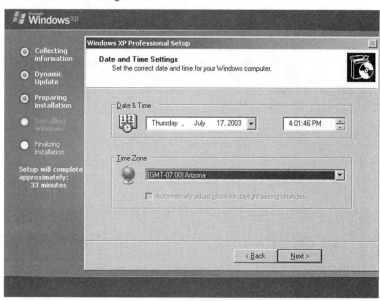

17. Enter the correct date and time. Then, select the correct time zone. Click **Next** to continue.

The next screen automatically installs the networking components. The setup process first installs the network, as shown in Figure B.21.

Figure B.21 Installing Network Screen

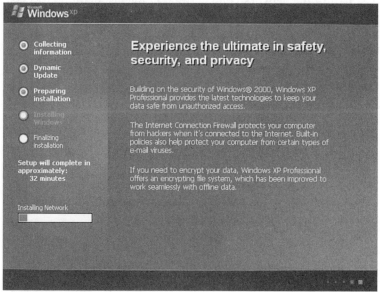

Next, it prompts you to choose the Typical or Custom settings, as shown in Figure B.22.

Figure B.22 Networking Settings Screen

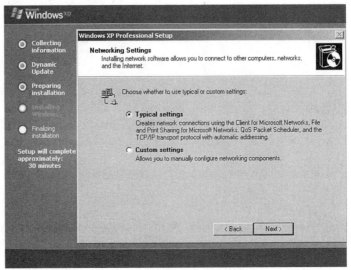

18. For the purposes of this lab, select **Typical settings**. This selection is the most common selection and automatically configures the network settings. If you choose the Custom setting, you must manually configure the networking components. Click **Next** to continue to the next step.

The last part of the network configuration in the installation process involves assigning workgroup or domain membership (see Figure B.23).

Figure B.23 Workgroup or Computer Domain Screen

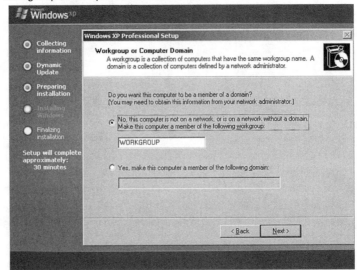

The Workgroup or Computer Domain screen allows you to join a domain. This step is important when the computer is on a network and it requires a domain name and password.

19. Select **No, This Computer Is Not on a Network, or Is on a Network Without a Domain Radio Button.** Then, click the **Next** button.

   This step completes the user involvement in the setup of the installation process. It is the final step of the setup process. This step takes the longest to complete. Once it finishes, click **Next**.

   The next steps are all automated, and they proceed through copying files, as shown in Figure B.24.

Figure B.24 Copying Files Screen

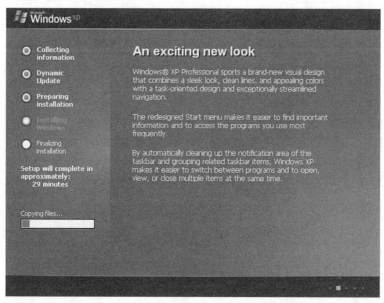

20. Setup completes the installation process, as shown in Figure B.25.

Figure B.25 Completing Installation Screen

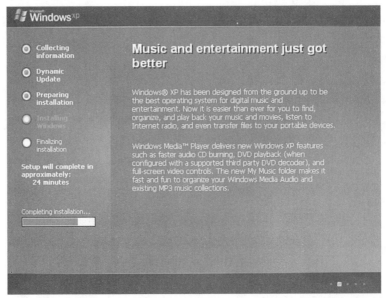

21. Setup installs the Start menu items, as shown in Figure B.26.

Figure B.26 Installing Start Menu Items Screen

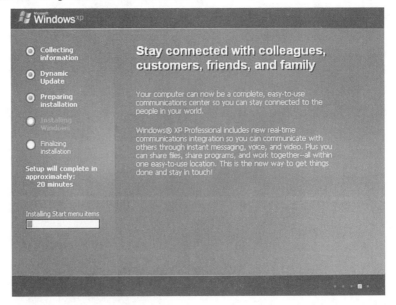

22. Next, setup registers components, as shown in Figure B.27.

Figure B.27 Registering Components Screen

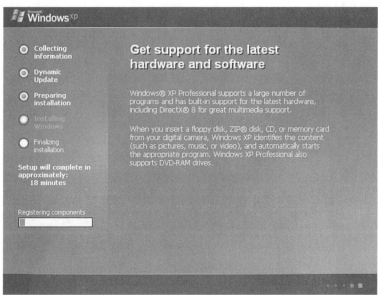

23. Setup finalizes the installation and saves the configuration settings, as shown in Figure B.28.

Figure B.28 Saving Settings Screen

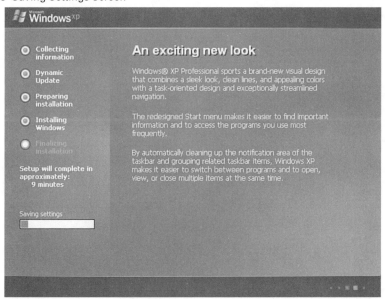

24. At this point, the computer automatically restarts. Ignore the **Press any Key to Boot from CD** message. Do not boot from the CD again.

25. The log on box appears, as shown in Figure B.29. Log on with the Administrator account and password that you created during setup.

Figure B.29 Log On Screen

26. The system now logs on and launches the Windows XP Professional desktop, as shown in Figure B.30.

Figure B.30 Windows XP Professional Desktop

Windows XP is now successfully installed.

Troubleshooting

Before beginning the installation, confirm the proper hardware requirements of the system. Also, make sure that you are installing the operating system on a blank partition or hard drive that has enough space. If the hardware is compatible and there is sufficient space on the drive or partition, you should not encounter any problems with the installation.

Reflection

Did the Windows installation complete successfully?

Answers—Lab B-1: Installation Demonstration of Windows XP

Step 1

This step does not require a specific answer.

Reflection

Did your Windows installation complete successfully?

The answer should be yes. If not, you must review all of the steps and possibly do another install.

Lab B-2: Using Simple File Sharing to Share Files

Estimated Time: 30 Minutes

Objective

In this lab, you use the Simple File Sharing techniques and tools that are new to Windows XP. This lab helps you become familiar with the easy and simplified method for sharing resources in a Windows XP network.

Equipment

You need the following equipment for this lab:

- A computer with Windows XP Professional Edition installed

Scenario

The IT department has purchased some computers with Windows XP Professional Edition as the operating system on the machines. It wants you to learn how to share files in the file system so you can help other employees.

Procedures

You can share files in the Windows XP Professional Edition file system in the same way you did with Windows 2000; however, Windows XP Professional Edition added a few extra features for file sharing that make this process a little easier, faster, and more user friendly. This lab will show you how to use these new features.

Step 1

The first step of this lab shows you how to turn on the file-sharing feature. File sharing is turned on by default in Windows XP:

1. First, click **Start** (the Start menu) and then click **My Documents** to open the window.

2. Next, click the **Tools** button on the menu list at the top of the screen. Then, scroll down and select **folder options**. This step opens the folder options dialog box.

3. Click the **View** tab. This step allows you to select various advanced folder settings. Scroll through these options and read them to become familiar with some of the options and what they do. At the bottom, you see the **Use Simple File Sharing (Recommended)** setting.

4. The Simple File Sharing radio button should be checked because it is the default setting. If you decide at a later date that you do not want to use simple file sharing, you uncheck this radio box to disable it.

5. Click the **OK** button to close the folder options box.

Step 2

For this step, leave the My Documents window open. Create a new folder called **Shared Files** within My Documents. This step uses Simple File Sharing to share a folder with other users who have local user accounts on that computer:

1. Right-click an open area of the My Documents window and select **New > Folder**. The new folder appears in the My Documents window. Rename it **Shared Files**.

2. Next, right-click the Shared Files folder and select **Properties**. This move opens the properties dialog box for the Shared Files folder. Choose the **Sharing** tab.

Read both the Local Sharing and Security and Network Sharing and Security sections to understand the available options.

3. Do not choose the Make This Folder Private radio box because it disables access to the folder. Instead, drag this folder to the **Shared Documents** folder to share the Shared Files folder.

4. Click **OK** to close the properties box of the Shared Files folder. Now, locate the Shared Documents folder on the left panel of the My Documents folder. To drag the Shared Files folder to this folder, click the Shared Files folder and hold it down while dragging it over to the **Shared Documents** folder.

5. Now, click the **Shared Documents** link on the left panel. Once this folder opens, the Shared Files folder will be in there. Other users who have local accounts on this computer will be able to access any files that you put into the Shared Files folders.

    If you decide that you do not want to share the folder or files, simply delete them from this folder.

Step 3

For this step, leave the My Documents window open. Use the existing Shared Files folder to share:

1. First, right-click the Shared Files folder and select **Properties**. This step opens the properties dialog box for the Shared Files folder. Choose the **Sharing** tab. Read both the Local Sharing and Security and Network Sharing and Security sections to understand the options.

2. On the Network Sharing and Security section, click the link that states that you understand the implications of sharing this item on the network. Then, select the **Just Enable File Sharing** radio box. Sometimes, this step is necessary if you see only a **Share This Folder on the Network** box, which can be selected. Select this box and click **Apply**.

3. Next, click the **OK** button. Now, other users who have access to the network workgroup or domain can access files located within this folder.

4. Look at the Shared Files folder. There should be a little hand holding the folder. This hand indicates that the folder is being shared on the network.

Reflection

You just learned how to use Windows XP's Simple File Sharing tool to share files locally on the computer and across the network. In what ways is this easier or better than the more traditional way of doing it Windows 2000? How might it be worse? What are some of the advantages of using the traditional way of sharing files?

_____

_____

_____

_____

_____

_____

Answers—Lab B-2: Using Simple File Sharing to Share Files

Reflection

Answers to this question vary. Answers to the first part of the reflection question should be that using Simple File Sharing is a lot easier and more user friendly. The permissions settings are handled automatically for you. This arrangement is good for someone who might not be familiar with how permissions work. Answers to the second part should be that using the traditional method is better for maintaining control and customization over assigning permissions. It provides more flexibility on adding or denying specific users or groups permissions. It also lets you apply more specific permissions other than just sharing the resource or not, which is essentially what Simple File Sharing does. Which method depends on the environment and user who administers the security of the computer or network?

Lab B-3: Remote Desktop Connection

Estimated Time: 30 Minutes

Objective

In this lab, you use Windows XP's Remote Desktop Connection to establish a remote connection to another computer.

Equipment

You need the following equipment for this lab:

- Two computer systems with Windows XP Professional Edition installed

Scenario

You are the system administrator for the XYZ Company. You have just upgraded some of the client PCs on the network to Windows XP Professional Edition. You want to set up the client PCs for Remote Desktop Administration. This move enables the IT department to provide desktop support remotely.

Procedures

Before beginning this lab, set up two computers so that they are connected. Make sure that they can communicate or ping each other. Gather the IP configuration data from both PCs. The first part of the lab shows how to set up the remote computer (which will be the computer that you administer remotely). The second part of the lab shows how to set up the client computer (which will be the computer that you are making the remote connection from).

Step 1

1. Enable Remote Desktop on the remote computer. Next, gather the IP information and record it for Step 2.

2. Log on with the administrator account or as a user that is a member of the Administrator group.

3. Open the Control Panel and then locate and double-click the **System** icon. In the **System Properties** dialog box, click the **Remote** tab.

4. Under the Remote Desktop section, select **Allow Users to Connect Remotely to This Computer**.

5. Click the **Select Remote Users** button to change who has permission to remotely connect to the computer.

6. Next, select **Add**. In the empty box, type the username of the account that is used to log into the computer and select **OK**.

7. Now, gather the IP information. To do so, choose **Start > Run**. Type **cmd** and then click **OK**. At the DOS prompt, type **ipconfig /all**. You see the IP configuration for the computer. Write down the host name and IP address. Keep this information for Step 2.

   At this point, the remote computer is set up to receive incoming remote connections.

NOTE

As long as an account has a logon password and that account is logged on, the user can remotely connect to the computer. The administrator or any user who is a member of the Administrator or local Remote Desktop Users group can remotely connect to the computer as well.

Step 2

It is important to note that a user doesn't have to be using Windows XP Professional on the client computer to remotely connect to the remote computer. However, the remote computer must be running Windows XP Professional Edition, regardless of what version of Windows the client computer is running. In some cases, such as when the remote computer is running Windows 2000 Server or Advanced Server, you can turn on Terminal Services to remotely administer the server. For this course, Windows 2000 Professional Edition does not have Terminal Services and therefore cannot be the remote computer:

1. Open the Start menu and select All Programs > Accessories > Communications > Remote Desktop Connection.

2. Type in the IP address of the remote computer that you recorded in Step 1. Then, click the **Options** tab.

3. In the username space, type the username of the account that has administrative access to the remote computer.

4. Next, click **Connect**. At this point, the client computer attempts to make a connection. When a connection is made, a logon screen appears. The username should be there. Type in the password, and then click the **OK** button.

Step 3

If the client computer is using a operating system other than Windows XP Professional, it can still remotely connect to a Windows XP system. To do so, install the files from the Windows XP Professional Edition installation CD:

1. Insert the CD into the CD-ROM drive. When the XP menu appears, select **Perform Additional Tasks** and then select **Set Up Remote Desktop Connection**.

2. The necessary files are copied to the hard drive and the setup process finishes.

3. To make the remote connection, simply follow the steps in Step 2 of this lab.

Troubleshooting

For the computers to be able to connect to each other, they must be able to establish contact, communicate, and find each other on the network prior to running Remote Desktop Connection. You can begin the process by gathering and recording the IP configurations for both computers by typing **ipconfig /all** at the command prompt. Use the **ping** command to establish that the computers will be able to connect when using Remote Desktop Connection.

Reflection

Use the Remote Desktop Connection utility to connect to your work computer from home. This process requires a more advanced knowledge of computer networking because it involves establishing a virtual private network (VPN) through the Internet, and you must configure the routers and firewalls on both ends to open the proper port numbers to establish a remote connection. Windows XP also provides a means of making a Remote Desktop Connection to your PC through the Internet over a web connection.

1. What are some advantages of using Remote Desktop Connection?

   _____

   _____

2. What are some disadvantages or security concerns when using Remote Desktop Connection?

   _____

   _____

Answers—Lab B-3: Remote Desktop Connection

Reflection

1. Answers to the first question should be that Remote Desktop Connection makes it easier for IT departments to support end users by being able to remotely control the computer and troubleshoot the problem. Also, it enables system administrators to control centralized servers from a remote location. Home users benefit because they can access the home computer from work.

2. Security concerns include leaving open the remote desktop connection port, means the computer is vulnerable to people who have the username and password.

Lab B-4: Internet Connection Firewall

Estimated Time: 30 Minutes

Objective

In this lab, you learn how to use the integrated firewall that is included with the latest releases of Microsoft's operating systems, including Windows XP. You select the proper settings, which allows a user or administrator to secure the operating system from intruders.

Equipment

You need the following equipment for this lab:

- A computer system running Windows XP

Scenario

The IT department has purchased some new computers with Windows XP installed on them. These new computers are going to be used by people in the finance and accounting departments of the company. It is important that these computers be as secure as possible and that all the data be protected from intruders. Although proper firewalls, filters, and access lists have been placed on the corporate network's incoming gateways, these computers need to be secure from internal threats and intruders within the network boundaries. The IT department manager has instructed you to implement Windows XP's integrated firewall on these computers to block them from intruders.

Procedures

Before beginning this lab, you need to be logged in as the administrator or a member of the administrators group. It is important to understand that the management tasks we cover in this lab apply to other computers that are part of the network, and these settings affect only the individual computer you configure them on.

Step 1

The first step in configuring the Windows XP integrated firewall is to locate and open the Network and Internet Connections settings in the Control Panel:

1. Open the Control Panel using the Start menu. Click the **Start** button. Then, click the **Control Panel** button to open the Control Panel.

2. Double-click the **Network Connection** icon in the Control Panel to open the dialog box.

3. Click the **Local Area Connection** icon to reveal the list of network tasks on the left side of the network connection screen.

Step 2

In Step 2, you learn about various settings and how to open the Integrated Firewall Settings dialog box:

1. Click **View Status of This Connection**.

2. On the General tab, you can see the various status settings related to the network connection, such as status, duration, and speed. You can also disable the network connection by clicking the Disable button; however, do not do so in this lab.

3. Next, click the **Support** tab. This area shows you useful information about the network connection, such as the address type, IP address, subnet mask, and default gateway. Using this information and the information from the previous step helps you determine what sort of firewall settings to select, which you do in the next section of this lab.

Step 3

In this step, you configure the proper Internet Connection Firewall (ICF) settings for this computer:

1. First, click back on the **General** tab and then click the **Properties** button. You see the Local Area Connection Properties dialog box, where you can make various configurations and settings on the network connection.

2. Next, click the **Advanced** tab in the Local Area Connection Properties dialog box. At this point, you should see the ICF settings. The first thing you might want to do is click the Learn More About Internet Connection Firewall link. This move opens a page that contains further documentation about the Windows XP ICF.

3. After reading the material, close that page and return to the Local Area Connection Properties dialog box. Click the check box next to the **Protect My Computer and Network by Limiting or Preventing Access to This Computer from the Internet.**

4. You see a Settings button appear in the bottom-right corner of the Local Area Connection Properties dialog box. Click this button to bring up the ICF Advanced Settings screen.

   This screen has three tabs. First, you must configure the Services tab.

5. Click the **Services** tab. Select all the boxes that you see. As you select each one, a pop-up box allows you to select the name or IP address of the computer that is hosting these services on the network. If this were an actual production environment instead of a lab, you would put the correct hostname of the computer that is hosting these services on the network. Also note the internal and external port number on these pop-up windows. They are the actual ports numbers that will be closed when you click these boxes. By clicking all these boxes, you are essentially closing most of the well-known or popular ports that intruders can use to access the computer. If this computer were acting as a gateway that other computers used to gain Internet access, closing these ports would also disable the access to the other computers that use this computer as a gateway.

6. Click the **Security Logging** tab. This tab allows you to log events such as attempts or connections made to the computer.

7. Click both the **Log Dropped Packets** and **Log Successful Connections** boxes to enable security logging.

8. Next, click the **ICMP** tab. Internet Control Message Protocol (ICMP) is commonly used for error-checking and testing connectivity of remote computers. Sometimes, intruders or hackers use ICMP to access or damage remote computers. Using this tab, it is possible to disable ICMP events or connections from being received and interpreted by this computer.

9. Select all the boxes in the ICMP tab window. Notice as you select them, descriptions of these various ICMP tasks appear at the bottom of the ICMP tab window. Read them as you select them to become more familiar which what each one does.

10. After you select all the boxes, click the **OK** button to save these settings and close the ICF settings box. Then, click **OK** on the Local Area Connection Properties dialog box to save the settings and close that box. Also, click the **Close** button on the Local Area Connection Status dialog box to close it. Close the Network Connection window that you opened in the Control Panel.

You have now successfully configured the ICF in Windows XP.

Troubleshooting

Sometimes, when you configure these settings, they tighten or shut off too much access and actually prohibit users from doing their jobs or accessing network resources that they otherwise need. In this case, it might be necessary to tweak these ICF settings so that users have the access they require. Pay careful attention whenever configuring any type of firewall or security settings.

Reflection

What other security tasks would you have to address to help protect a computer besides using the ICF?

_____

_____

_____

Answers—Lab B-4: Internet Connection Firewall

Reflection

Answers to this question vary because you can take numerous security measures to protect a computer. Answers to this question can include such things as password protection or security permissions on shared resources.

Lab B-5: Using Windows XP's Start Menu and Windows Explorer

Estimated Time: 30 Minutes

Objective

You explore the basic features of the Windows XP Start menu and Windows Explorer Navigation tools.

Equipment

You need the following equipment for this lab:

- A computer system with Windows XP Professional Edition installed

Scenario

The IT department of XYZ Company has installed a computer with Windows XP Professional Edition. The company has asked you to run a few tasks to explore the features of the Start menu to ensure that it is running properly. It also wants you to learn to navigate the file system so that you can help other employees.

Procedures

Before beginning this lab, make sure that the Windows XP machine is powered on and you can log in. Windows XP Professional Edition has many new features. Some features such as the Start menu and Control Panel have undergone drastic changes. These changes might make the features difficult to use the first time someone uses a graphical user interface (GUI). You navigate the Windows XP Professional Edition file system in almost the same way you did with Windows 2000; however, Windows XP Professional Edition added a few extra features that help in navigating the file system easier and faster. This lab will show you how to use the new features of Windows XP to navigate the file system.

Part I: Using the Windows XP Start Menu

Step 1

1. Once the system boots, the Windows XP Welcome Screen appears. Click the proper **username** and then log in with the password.

2. When finished entering the password, press **Enter.** If you typed the password correctly, the system authenticates you and grants you access.

Step 2

1. After the system authenticates the user, the desktop environment appears, as shown in Figure B.31.

Figure B.31 Windows XP Professional Desktop

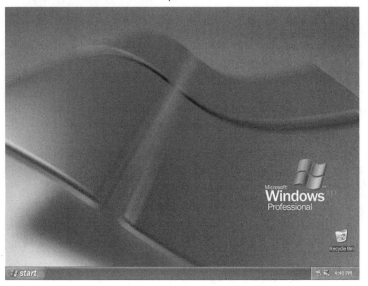

2. Notice that the Windows XP Professional desktop environment is different from Windows 2000. By default, the My Computer, My Documents, My Network Places, and Internet Explorer icons do not appear on the desktop. You can enable these icons to appear on the desktop if you want. You do so later in the lab.

Step 3

Using the new XP Start menu can be a little confusing the first time. However, once you become familiar with the new Start menu, you will see that the changes Microsoft made will help you navigate the GUI more easily. The following tasks help you become familiar with the new Start menu:

1. To get an idea of what the new Start menu looks like, click the **Start menu** icon in the bottom-left corner of the screen. Notice that the icons that are missing from the desktop now appear in the Start menu. You also see that the Start menu is divided into two parts. The left side shows a list of the programs that you use frequently. The right side shows what is in My Computer and My Network Places. It also contains the Control Panel, Printers and Faxes, and the Search and Run function icons.

2. Click a few of the programs and open up a few windows to simulate a typical environment that a user would have when working on the computer.

3. Now, access My Computer by using the Start menu. Click the **Start** icon, and then click the **My Computer** icon. So you don't have to close all the windows and then click the icon on the desktop, it appears in the Start menu; you can access it much more quickly.

4. Now, examine some of the various options that are available to customize the Windows XP Start menu. First, right-click the **Start menu** icon and select **Properties**.

5. Next, click the **Taskbar** tab. You have several options to change how the Start menu and Taskbar work. Click some of the radio boxes to select or deselect certain options until the Start menu is the way you like it. When finished, click the **Start menu** tab.

6. Notice that Windows XP provides the option of using the Classic Start menu that came with previous releases of Microsoft Windows operating systems. Click the **Customize** button. This button provides a new interface to manipulate the Start menu. First, change the setting to use **Small Icons** rather than the large ones. Second, deselect the Internet and E-mail radio buttons located on the bottom of the dialog box. They will no longer appear in the Start menu. Remember, you can always go back and select these boxes if you want them to be quickly available in the Start menu.

7. Next, look at the Programs section of this screen; you can see that it is possible to change how many programs are available for quick selection on the Start menu. Change the amount to **11**, and then click **OK**. The first box should disappear. Click the **Apply** button and then the **OK** button. You should see the new changes on the Start menu.

8. Keep in mind that the more a user uses Windows XP, he or she learns that the majority of the GUI operations performed involve the Start menu as the starting place. Users will quickly learn that there is really no need to have any icons on the desktop. For those who like the icons on the desktop, Step 4 of this lab shows how to add the icons.

Step 4

1. Locate the mouse pointer on the desktop and right-click the mouse. Scroll down and click the **Properties** button. You see the system's Display Properties dialog box.

2. Next, select the **Desktop** tab. You see the menu that allows you to change the desktop feature.

3. Now, click the **Customize Desktop** button in the bottom-left corner of the properties box. A dialog box allows you to make further adjustments to the desktop. From this point, you can select which icons you want to display on the desktop. You can also change what the icon looks like or run the desktop-cleanup tool. The **Web** tab lets you display web pages on the desktop. You can also lock the desktop items to prevent someone from moving or resizing web items on the desktop.

Part II: Using the Windows XP Windows Explorer Navigation Tool

Step 1

The first feature that you want to know is how to navigate to any window without having to close windows or even using Windows Explorer:

1. Click the **Start menu** and then click **My Computer.** Notice how the icons are arranged differently?

2. First, click the **Tools** menu on the top of the screen and select **Folder Options.** After the Folder Options box opens, select the **View** tab. Then, scroll down until you come to Show Control Panel in My Computer and make sure it is checked. If it is not selected, select it because it is not checked by default. Next, click the **Apply** button. This step lets you have the Control Panel icon in the My Computer window.

Step 2

1. For this step, leave the My Computer window open. Look down the left side of the screen to see the Other Places menu. It shows the other directories that you can navigate to from this window without having to close the current window.

2. First, click the **My Documents** icon in the **Other Places** menu. It takes you to the My Documents window. Do the same thing to navigate back to the My Computer window or change to a different window from here as well.

3. Double-click the **C: drive** and open a folder. Use the **Other Places** menu to navigate to different folders and back again, all from one window.

4. Open the **Control Panel** from the Start menu. By default, the icons are grouped together by categories.

5. Now, choose an item from the **Control Panel** list such as **Performance and Maintenance.** You have the option of selecting one of the tasks from the list, or you can select one of the icons to compete a specific task.

Reflection

In what circumstances might this way of navigating the file system be easier?

_____

_____

_____

Answers—Lab B-5: Using Windows XP's Start Menu and Windows Explorer

Reflection

Navigating the file system using the methods in this lab is easier because everything is accessible from one screen. From one screen, you can go wherever you need to access any file or program without having to open additional windows or file menus.

Index